DATE DUE

No Exit

AND

The Flies

No Exit & The Flies

(Huis Clos)   (Les Mouches)

A PLAY IN ONE ACT   **A PLAY IN THREE ACTS**

BY

Jean-Paul Sartre

English versions by STUART GILBERT

1977   *ALFRED A. KNOPF*   *New York*

THIS IS A BORZOI BOOK,
PUBLISHED BY ALFRED A. KNOPF, INC.

Published February 20, 1947
Reprinted Twelve Times
Fourteenth Printing, July 1977

CONTENTS

NO EXIT

(*Huis Clos*)

❖❖❖

A PLAY IN ONE ACT

CHARACTERS IN THE PLAY

VALET

GARCIN

ESTELLE

INEZ

Huis Clos (*No Exit*) was presented for the first time at the Théâtre du Vieux-Colombier, Paris, in May 1944.

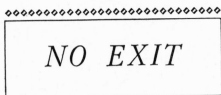

NO EXIT

SCENE

A drawing-room in Second Empire style. A massive bronze ornament stands on the mantelpiece.

GARCIN [*enters, accompanied by the* ROOM-VALET, *and glances around him*]: Hm! So here we are?

VALET: Yes, Mr. Garcin.

GARCIN: And this is what it looks like?

VALET: Yes.

GARCIN: Second Empire furniture, I observe. . . . Well, well, I dare say one gets used to it in time.

VALET: Some do. Some don't.

GARCIN: Are all the other rooms like this one?

VALET: How could they be? We cater for all sorts: Chinamen and Indians, for instance. What use would they have for a Second Empire chair?

GARCIN: And what use do you suppose *I* have for one? Do you know who I was? . . . Oh, well, it's no great matter. And, to tell the truth, I had quite a habit of living among furniture that I didn't relish, and in false positions. I'd even come to like it. A false position in a Louis-Philippe dining-room—you know the style?—well, that had its points, you know. Bogus in bogus, so to speak.

VALET: And you'll find that living in a Second Empire drawing-room has its points.

GARCIN: Really? . . . Yes, yes, I dare say. . . . [*He takes another look around.*] Still, I certainly didn't expect—this! You know what they tell us down there?

VALET: What about?

GARCIN: About [*makes a sweeping gesture*] this—er —residence.

VALET: Really, sir, how could you believe such cock-and-bull stories? Told by people who'd never set foot here. For, of course, if they had—

GARCIN: Quite so. [*Both laugh. Abruptly the laugh dies from* GARCIN's *face.*] But, I say, where are the instruments of torture?

VALET: The what?

GARCIN: The racks and red-hot pincers and all the other paraphernalia?

VALET: Ah, you must have your little joke, sir!

GARCIN: My little joke? Oh, I see. No, I wasn't joking. [*A short silence. He strolls round the room.*] No mirrors, I notice. No windows. Only to be expected. And nothing breakable. [*Bursts out angrily.*] But, damn it all, they might have left me my toothbrush!

VALET: That's good! So you haven't yet got over your —what-do-you-call-it?—sense of human dignity? Excuse me smiling.

◇◇

GARCIN [*thumping ragefully the arm of an arm-chair*] : I'll ask you to be more polite. I quite realize the position I'm in, but I won't tolerate . . .

VALET : Sorry, sir. No offense meant. But all our guests ask me the same questions. Silly questions, if you'll pardon me saying so. Where's the torture-chamber ? That's the first thing they ask, all of them. They don't bother their heads about the bathroom requisites, that I can assure you. But after a bit, when they've got their nerve back, they start in about their toothbrushes and what-not. Good heavens, Mr. Garcin, can't you use your brains ? What, I ask you, would be the point of brushing your teeth ?

GARCIN [*more calmly*] : Yes, of course you're right. [*He looks around again.*] And why should one want to see oneself in a looking-glass ? But that bronze contraption on the mantelpiece, that's another story. I suppose there will be times when I stare my eyes out at it. Stare my eyes out—see what I mean ? . . . All right, let's put our cards on the table. I assure you I'm quite conscious of my position. Shall I tell you what it feels like ? A man's drowning, choking, sinking by inches, till only his eyes are just above water. And what does he see ? A bronze atrocity by —what's the fellow's name ?—Barbedienne. A collector's piece. As in a nightmare. That's their idea, isn't it ? . . . No, I suppose you're under orders not to answer questions; and I won't insist. But don't forget, my man, I've a good notion of what's coming to me, so don't you boast you've caught me off my guard. I'm facing the situation, facing it. [*He starts pacing the room again.*] So that's that; no toothbrush. And no bed, either. One never sleeps, I take it?

VALET: That's so.

GARCIN: Just as I expected. *Why* should one sleep? A sort of drowsiness steals on you, tickles you behind the ears, and you feel your eyes closing—but why sleep? You lie down on the sofa and—in a flash, sleep flies away. Miles and miles away. So you rub your eyes, get up, and it starts all over again.

VALET: Romantic, that's what you are.

GARCIN: Will you keep quiet, please! . . . I won't make a scene, I shan't be sorry for myself, I'll face the situation, as I said just now. Face it fairly and squarely. I won't have it springing at me from behind, before I've time to size it up. And you call that being "romantic"! . . . So it comes to this; one doesn't need rest. Why bother about sleep if one isn't sleepy? That stands to reason, doesn't it? Wait a minute, there's a snag somewhere; something disagreeable. Why, now, should it be disagreeable? . . . Ah, I see; it's life without a break.

VALET: What do you mean by that?

GARCIN: What do I mean? [*Eyes the* VALET *suspiciously.*] I thought as much. That's why there's something so beastly, so damn bad-mannered, in the way you stare at me. They're paralyzed.

VALET: What are you talking about?

GARCIN: Your eyelids. We move ours up and down.

Blinking, we call it. It's like a small black shutter that clicks down and makes a break. Everything goes black; one's eyes are moistened. You can't imagine how restful, refreshing, it is. Four thousand little rests per hour. Four thousand little respites—just think! . . . So that's the idea. I'm to live without eyelids. Don't act the fool, you know what I mean. No eyelids, no sleep; it follows, doesn't it? I shall never sleep again. But then—how shall I endure my own company? Try to understand. You see, I'm fond of teasing, it's a second nature with me—and I'm used to teasing myself. Plaguing myself, if you prefer; I don't tease nicely. But I can't go on doing that without a break. Down there I had my nights. I slept. I always had good nights. By way of compensation, I suppose. And happy little dreams. There was a green field. Just an ordinary field. I used to stroll in it. . . . Is it daytime now?

VALET: Can't you see? The lights are on.

GARCIN: Ah yes, I've got it. It's *your* daytime. And outside?

VALET: Outside?

GARCIN: Damn it, you know what I mean. Beyond that wall.

VALET: There's a passage.

GARCIN: And at the end of the passage?

VALET: There's more rooms, more passages, and stairs.

GARCIN: And what lies beyond them?

VALET: That's all.

GARCIN: But surely you have a day off sometimes. Where do you go?

◇◇

VALET: To my uncle's place. He's the head valet here. He has a room on the third floor.

GARCIN: I should have guessed as much. Where's the light-switch?

VALET: There isn't any.

GARCIN: What? Can't one turn off the light?

VALET: Oh, the management can cut off the current if they want to. But I can't remember their having done so on this floor. We have all the electricity we want.

GARCIN: So one has to live with one's eyes open all the time?

VALET: To *live*, did you say?

GARCIN: Don't let's quibble over words. With one's eyes open. Forever. Always broad daylight in my eyes—and in my head. [*Short silence.*] And suppose I took that contraption on the mantelpiece and dropped it on the lamp—wouldn't it go out?

VALET: You can't move it. It's too heavy.

GARCIN [*seizing the bronze ornament and trying to lift it*]: You're right. It's too heavy.

[*A short silence follows.*]

VALET: Very well, sir, if you don't need me any more, I'll be off.

GARCIN: What? You're going? [*The* VALET *goes up to the door.*] Wait. [VALET *looks round.*] That's a bell, isn't it? [VALET *nods.*] And if I ring, you're bound to come?

VALET: Well, yes, that's so—in a way. But you can never be sure about that bell. There's something

wrong with the wiring, and it doesn't always work.
[GARCIN *goes to the bell-push and presses the but-*
ton. A bell purrs outside.]

GARCIN : It's working all right.

VALET [*looking surprised*] : So it is. [*He, too, presses*
the button.] But I shouldn't count on it too much if
I were you. It's—capricious. Well, I really must go
now. [GARCIN *makes a gesture to detain him.*] Yes,
sir?

GARCIN : No, never mind. [*He goes to the mantelpiece*
and picks up a paper-knife.] What's this?

VALET : Can't you see? An ordinary paper-knife.

GARCIN : Are there books here?

VALET : No.

GARCIN : Then what's the use of this? [VALET *shrugs*
his shoulders.] Very well. You can go. [VALET *goes*
out.]

[GARCIN *is by himself. He goes to the bronze orna-*
ment and strokes it reflectively. He sits down; then
gets up, goes to the bell-push, and presses the button.
The bell remains silent. He tries two or three times,
without success. Then he tries to open the door, also
without success. He calls the VALET *several times,*
but gets no result. He beats the door with his fists,
still calling. Suddenly he grows calm and sits down
again. At the same moment the door opens and INEZ
enters, followed by the VALET.]

VALET : Did you call, sir?

GARCIN [*on the point of answering "Yes"—but then*
his eyes fall on INEZ] : No.

VALET [*turning to* INEZ] : This is your room, madam.

[INEZ *says nothing.*] If there's any information you require—? [INEZ *still keeps silent, and the* VALET *looks slightly huffed.*] Most of our guests have quite a lot to ask me. But I won't insist. Anyhow, as regards the toothbrush, and the electric bell, and that thing on the mantelshelf, this gentleman can tell you anything you want to know as well as I could. We've had a little chat, him and me. [VALET *goes out.*] [GARCIN *refrains from looking at* INEZ, *who is inspecting the room. Abruptly she turns to* GARCIN.]

INEZ: Where's Florence? [GARCIN *does not reply.*] Didn't you hear? I asked you about Florence. Where is she?

GARCIN: I haven't an idea.

INEZ: Ah, that's the way it works, is it? Torture by separation. Well, as far as I'm concerned, you won't get anywhere. Florence was a tiresome little fool, and I shan't miss her in the least.

GARCIN: I beg your pardon. Who do you suppose I am?

INEZ: You? Why, the torturer, of course.

GARCIN [*looks startled, then bursts out laughing*]: Well, that's a good one! Too comic for words. I the torturer! So you came in, had a look at me, and thought I was—er—one of the staff. Of course, it's that silly fellow's fault; he should have introduced us. A torturer indeed! I'm Joseph Garcin, journalist and man of letters by profession. And as we're both in the same boat, so to speak, might I ask you, Mrs.—?

INEZ: [*testily*]: Not "Mrs." I'm unmarried.

GARCIN : Right. That's a start, anyway. Well, now that we've broken the ice, do you *really* think I look like a torturer? And, by the way, how does one recognize torturers when one sees them? Evidently you've ideas on the subject.

INEZ : They look frightened.

GARCIN : Frightened! But how ridiculous! Of whom should they be frightened? Of their victims?

INEZ : Laugh away, but I know what I'm talking about. I've often watched my face in the glass.

GARCIN : In the glass? [*He looks around him.*] How beastly of them! They've removed everything in the least resembling a glass. [*Short silence.*] Anyhow, I can assure you I'm not frightened. Not that I take my position lightly; I realize its gravity only too well. But I'm not afraid.

INEZ [*shrugging her shoulders*] : That's your affair. [*Silence.*] Must you be here all the time, or do you take a stroll outside, now and then?

GARCIN : The door's locked.

INEZ : Oh! . . . That's too bad.

GARCIN : I can quite understand that it bores you having me here. And I, too—well, quite frankly, I'd rather be alone. I want to think things out, you know; to set my life in order, and one does that better by oneself. But I'm sure we'll manage to pull along together somehow. I'm no talker, I don't move much; in fact I'm a peaceful sort of fellow. Only, if I may venture on a suggestion, we should make a point of being extremely courteous to each other. That will ease the situation for us both.

◇◇◇

INEZ : I'm not polite.

GARCIN : Then I must be polite for two.

[*A longish silence.* GARCIN *is sitting on a sofa, while* INEZ *paces up and down the room.*]

INEZ [*fixing her eyes on him*] : Your mouth!

GARCIN [*as if waking from a dream*] : I beg your pardon.

INEZ : Can't you keep your mouth still? You keep twisting it about all the time. It's grotesque.

GARCIN : So sorry. I wasn't aware of it.

INEZ : That's just what I reproach you with. [GARCIN's *mouth twitches.*] There you are! You talk about politeness, and you don't even try to control your face. Remember you're not alone; you've no right to inflict the sight of your fear on me.

GARCIN [*getting up and going towards her*] : How about you? Aren't you afraid?

INEZ : What would be the use? There was some point in being afraid *before;* while one still had hope.

GARCIN [*in a low voice*] : There's no more hope—but it's still "before." We haven't yet begun to suffer.

INEZ : That's so. [*A short silence.*] Well? What's going to happen?

GARCIN : I don't know. I'm waiting.

[*Silence again.* GARCIN *sits down and* INEZ *resumes her pacing up and down the room.* GARCIN's *mouth twitches; after a glance at* INEZ *he buries his face in his hands. Enter* ESTELLE *with the* VALET. ESTELLE *looks at* GARCIN, *whose face is still hidden by his hands.*]

ESTELLE [*to* GARCIN] : No! Don't look up. I know

◇◇

what you're hiding with your hands. I know you've no face left. [GARCIN *removes his hands.*] What! [*A short pause. Then, in a tone of surprise*] But I don't know you!

GARCIN : I'm not the torturer, madam.

ESTELLE : I never thought you were. I—I thought someone was trying to play a rather nasty trick on me. [*To the* VALET] Is anyone else coming?

VALET : No, madam. No one else is coming.

ESTELLE : Oh! Then we're to stay by ourselves, the three of us, this gentleman, this lady, and myself. [*She starts laughing.*]

GARCIN [*angrily*] : There's nothing to laugh about.

ESTELLE [*still laughing*] : It's those sofas. They're so hideous. And just look how they've been arranged. It makes me think of New Year's Day—when I used to visit that boring old aunt of mine, Aunt Mary. Her house is full of horrors like that. . . . I suppose each of us has a sofa of his own. Is that one mine? [*To the* VALET] But you can't expect me to sit on that one. It would be too horrible for words. I'm in pale blue and it's vivid green.

INEZ : Would you prefer mine?

ESTELLE : That claret-colored one, you mean? That's very sweet of you, but really—no, I don't think it'd be so much better. What's the good of worrying, anyhow? We've got to take what comes to us, and I'll stick to the green one. [*Pauses.*] The only one which might do, at a pinch, is that gentleman's. [*Another pause.*]

INEZ : Did you hear, Mr. Garcin?

GARCIN [*with a slight start*]: Oh—the sofa, you mean. So sorry. [*He rises.*] Please take it, madam.

ESTELLE: Thanks. [*She takes off her coat and drops it on the sofa. A short silence.*] Well, as we're to live together, I suppose we'd better introduce ourselves. My name's Rigault. Estelle Rigault. [GARCIN *bows and is going to announce his name, but* INEZ *steps in front of him.*]

INEZ: And I'm Inez Serrano. Very pleased to meet you.

GARCIN [*bowing again*]: Joseph Garcin.

VALET: Do you require me any longer?

ESTELLE: No, you can go. I'll ring when I want you. [*Exit* VALET, *with polite bows to everyone.*]

INEZ: You're very pretty. I wish we'd had some flowers to welcome you with.

ESTELLE: Flowers? Yes, I loved flowers. Only they'd fade so quickly here, wouldn't they? It's so stuffy. Oh, well, the great thing is to keep as cheerful as we can, don't you agree? Of course, you, too, are—

INEZ: Yes. Last week. What about you?

ESTELLE: I'm—quite recent. Yesterday. As a matter of fact, the ceremony's not quite over. [*Her tone is natural enough, but she seems to be seeing what she describes.*] The wind's blowing my sister's veil all over the place. She's trying her best to cry. Come, dear! Make another effort. That's better. Two tears, two little tears are twinkling under the black veil. Oh dear! What a sight Olga looks this morning! She's holding my sister's arm, helping her along. She's not crying, and I don't blame her; tears always mess one's face up, don't they? Olga was my bosom friend, you know.

INEZ: Did you suffer much?

ESTELLE: No. I was only half conscious, mostly.

INEZ: What was it?

ESTELLE: Pneumonia. [*In the same tone as before*] It's over now, they're leaving the cemetery. Good-by. Good-by. Quite a crowd they are. My husband's stayed at home. Prostrated with grief, poor man. [*To* INEZ] How about you?

INEZ: The gas stove.

ESTELLE: And you, Mr. Garcin?

GARCIN: Twelve bullets through my chest. [ESTELLE *makes a horrified gesture.*] Sorry! I fear I'm not good company among the dead.

ESTELLE: Please, please don't use that word. It's so—so crude. In terribly bad taste, really. It doesn't mean much, anyhow. Somehow I feel we've never been so much alive as now. If we've absolutely got to mention this—this state of things, I suggest we call ourselves—wait!—absentees. Have you been—been absent for long?

GARCIN: About a month.

ESTELLE: Where do you come from?

GARCIN: From Rio.

ESTELLE: I'm from Paris. Have you anyone left down there?

GARCIN: Yes, my wife. [*In the same tone as* ESTELLE *has been using*] She's waiting at the entrance of the barracks. She comes there every day. But they won't let her in. Now she's trying to peep between the

◇◇

bars. She doesn't yet know I'm—absent, but she suspects it. Now she's going away. She's wearing her black dress. So much the better, she won't need to change. She isn't crying, but she never did cry, anyhow. It's a bright sunny day and she's like a black shadow creeping down the empty street. Those big tragic eyes of hers—with that martyred look they always had. Oh, how she got on my nerves!

[*A short silence.* GARCIN *sits on the central sofa and buries his head in his hands.*]

INEZ : Estelle!

ESTELLE : Please, Mr. Garcin!

GARCIN : What is it?

ESTELLE : You're sitting on my sofa.

GARCIN : I beg your pardon. [*He gets up.*]

ESTELLE : You looked so—so far away. Sorry I disturbed you.

GARCIN : I was setting my life in order. [INEZ *starts laughing.*] You may laugh, but you'd do better to follow my example.

INEZ : No need. My life's in perfect order. It tidied itself up nicely of its own accord. So I needn't bother about it now.

GARCIN : Really? You imagine it's so simple as that. [*He runs his hand over his forehead.*] Whew! How hot it is here! Do you mind if—? [*He begins taking off his coat.*]

ESTELLE : How dare you! [*More gently*] No, please don't. I loathe men in their shirt-sleeves.

GARCIN [*putting on his coat again*] : All right. [*A short pause.*] Of course, I used to spend my nights in the newspaper office, and it was a regular Black Hole, so we never kept our coats on. Stiflingly hot it could be. [*Short pause. In the same tone as previously*] Stifling, that it *is*. It's night now.

ESTELLE : That's so. Olga's undressing; it must be after midnight. How quickly the time passes, on earth!

INEZ : Yes, after midnight. They've sealed up my room. It's dark, pitch-dark, and empty.

GARCIN : They've slung their coats on the backs of the chairs and rolled up their shirt-sleeves above the elbow. The air stinks of men and cigar-smoke. [*A short silence.*] I used to like living among men in their shirt-sleeves.

ESTELLE [*aggressively*] : Well, in that case our tastes differ. That's all it proves. [*Turning to* INEZ] What about you? Do you like men in their shirt-sleeves?

INEZ : Oh, I don't care much for men any way.

ESTELLE [*looking at the other two with a puzzled air*] : Really I can't imagine why they put us three together. It doesn't make sense.

INEZ [*stifling a laugh*] : What's that you said?

ESTELLE : I'm looking at you two and thinking that we're going to live together. . . . It's so absurd. I expected to meet old friends, or relatives.

INEZ : Yes, a charming old friend—with a hole in the middle of his face.

ESTELLE : Yes, him too. He danced the tango so divinely. Like a professional. . . . But why, why should we of all people be put together?

◇◇

GARCIN : A pure fluke, I should say. They lodge folks as they can, in the order of their coming. [*To* INEZ] Why are you laughing?

INEZ : Because you amuse me, with your "flukes." As if they left anything to chance! But I suppose you've got to reassure yourself somehow.

ESTELLE [*hesitantly*] : I wonder, now. Don't you think we may have met each other at some time in our lives?

INEZ : Never. I shouldn't have forgotten you.

ESTELLE : Or perhaps we have friends in common. I wonder if you know the Dubois-Seymours?

INEZ : Not likely.

ESTELLE : But *everyone* went to their parties.

INEZ : What's their job?

ESTELLE : Oh, they don't do anything. But they have a lovely house in the country, and hosts of people visit them.

INEZ : I didn't. I was a post-office clerk.

ESTELLE [*recoiling a little*] : Ah, yes. . . . Of course, in that case— [*A pause.*] And you, Mr. Garcin?

GARCIN : We've never met. I always lived in Rio.

ESTELLE : Then you must be right. It's mere chance that has brought us together.

INEZ : Mere chance? Then it's by chance this room is furnished as we see it. It's an accident that the sofa on the right is a livid green, and that one on the left's wine-red. Mere chance? Well, just try to shift the sofas and you'll see the difference quick enough. And that statue on the mantelpiece, do you think it's there by accident? And what about the heat here?

How about that? [*A short silence.*] I tell you they've thought it all out. Down to the last detail. Nothing was left to chance. This room was all set for us.

ESTELLE: But really! Everything here's so hideous; all in angles, so uncomfortable. I always loathed angles.

INEZ [*shrugging her shoulders*]: And do you think *I* lived in a Second Empire drawing-room?

ESTELLE: So it was all fixed up beforehand?

INEZ: Yes. And they've put us together deliberately.

ESTELLE: Then it's not mere chance that *you* precisely are sitting opposite *me*? But what can be the idea behind it?

INEZ: Ask me another! I only know they're waiting.

ESTELLE: I never could bear the idea of anyone's expecting something from me. It always made me want to do just the opposite.

INEZ: Well, do it. Do it if you can. You don't even know what they expect.

ESTELLE [*stamping her foot*]: It's outrageous! So something's coming to me from you two? [*She eyes each in turn.*] Something nasty, I suppose. There are some faces that tell me everything at once. Yours don't convey anything.

GARCIN [*turning abruptly towards* INEZ]: Look here! Why are we together? You've given us quite enough hints, you may as well come out with it.

INEZ [*in a surprised tone*]: But I know nothing, absolutely nothing about it. I'm as much in the dark as you are.

GARCIN: We've *got* to know. [*Ponders for a while.*]

◇◇

INEZ : If only each of us had the guts to tell—

GARCIN : Tell what?

INEZ : Estelle!

ESTELLE : Yes?

INEZ : What have you done? I mean, why have they sent you here?

ESTELLE [*quickly*] : That's just it. I haven't a notion, not the foggiest. In fact, I'm wondering if there hasn't been some ghastly mistake. [*To* INEZ] Don't smile. Just think of the number of people who—who become absentees every day. There must be thousands and thousands, and probably they're sorted out by—by understrappers, you know what I mean. Stupid employees who don't know their job. So they're bound to make mistakes sometimes. . . . Do stop smiling. [*To* GARCIN] Why don't you speak? If they made a mistake in my case, they may have done the same about you. [*To* INEZ] And you, too. Anyhow, isn't it better to think we've got here by mistake?

INEZ : Is that all you have to tell us?

ESTELLE : What else should I tell? I've nothing to hide. I lost my parents when I was a kid, and I had my young brother to bring up. We were terribly poor and when an old friend of my people asked me to marry him I said yes. He was very well off, and quite nice. My brother was a very delicate child and needed all sorts of attention, so really that was the right thing for me to do, don't you agree? My husband was old enough to be my father, but for six

◇◇

years we had a happy married life. Then two years ago I met the man I was fated to love. We knew it the moment we set eyes on each other. He asked me to run away with him, and I refused. Then I got pneumonia and it finished me. That's the whole story. No doubt, by certain standards, I did wrong to sacrifice my youth to a man nearly three times my age. [*To* GARCIN] Do *you* think that could be called a sin?

GARCIN: Certainly not. [*A short silence.*] And now, tell me, do you think it's a crime to stand by one's principles?

ESTELLE: Of course not. Surely no one could blame a man for that!

GARCIN: Wait a bit! I ran a pacifist newspaper. Then war broke out. What was I to do? Everyone was watching me, wondering: "Will he dare?" Well, I dared. I folded my arms and they shot me. Had I done anything wrong?

ESTELLE [*laying her hand on his arm*]: Wrong? On the contrary. You were—

INEZ [*breaks in ironically*]: —a hero! And how about your wife, Mr. Garcin?

GARCIN: That's simple. I'd rescued her from—from the gutter.

ESTELLE [*to Inez*]: You see! You see!

INEZ: Yes, I see. [*A pause.*] Look here! What's the point of play-acting, trying to throw dust in each other's eyes? We're all tarred with the same brush.

ESTELLE [*indignantly*]: How dare you!

◇◇

INEZ : Yes, we are criminals—murderers—all three of us. We're in hell, my pets; they never make mistakes, and people aren't damned for nothing.

ESTELLE : Stop ! For heaven's sake—

INEZ : In hell ! Damned souls—that's us, all three !

ESTELLE : Keep quiet ! I forbid you to use such disgusting words.

INEZ : A damned soul—that's you, my little plaster saint. And ditto our friend there, the noble pacifist. We've had our hour of pleasure, haven't we ? There have been people who burned their lives out for our sakes—and we chuckled over it. So now we have to pay the reckoning.

GARCIN [*raising his fist*] : Will you keep your mouth shut, damn it !

INEZ [*confronting him fearlessly, but with a look of vast surprise*] : Well, well ! [*A pause.*] Ah, I understand now. I know why they've put us three together.

GARCIN : I advise you to—to think twice before you say any more.

INEZ : Wait ! You'll see how simple it is. Childishly simple. Obviously there aren't any physical torments —you agree, don't you ? And yet we're in hell. And no one else will come here. We'll stay in this room together, the three of us, for ever and ever. . . . In short, there's someone absent here, the official torturer.

GARCIN [*sotto voce*] : I'd noticed that.

INEZ : It's obvious what they're after—an economy of man-power—or devil-power, if you prefer. The same idea as in the cafeteria, where customers serve themselves.

ESTELLE: What ever do you mean?

INEZ: I mean that each of us will act as torturer of the two others.

[*There is a short silence while they digest this information.*]

GARCIN [*gently*]: No, I shall never be your torturer. I wish neither of you any harm, and I've no concern with you. None at all. So the solution's easy enough; each of us stays put in his or her corner and takes no notice of the others. You here, you here, and I there. Like soldiers at our posts. Also, we mustn't speak. Not one word. That won't be difficult; each of us has plenty of material for self-communings. I think I could stay ten thousand years with only my thoughts for company.

ESTELLE: Have *I* got to keep silent, too?

GARCIN: Yes. And that way we—we'll work out our salvation. Looking into ourselves, never raising our heads. Agreed?

INEZ: Agreed.

ESTELLE [*after some hesitation*]: I agree.

GARCIN: Then—good-by.

[*He goes to his sofa and buries his head in his hands. There is a long silence; then INEZ begins singing to herself.*]

INEZ [*singing*]:

> What a crowd in Whitefriars Lane!
> They've set trestles in a row,

◇◇◇

With a scaffold and the knife,
And a pail of bran below.
Come, good folks, to Whitefriars Lane,
Come to see the merry show!

The headsman rose at crack of dawn,
He'd a long day's work in hand,
Chopping heads off generals,
Priests and peers and admirals,
All the highest in the land.
What a crowd in Whitefriars Lane!

See them standing in a line,
Ladies all dressed up so fine.
But their heads have got to go,
Heads and hats roll down below.
Come, good folks, to Whitefriars Lane,
Come to see the merry show!

[*Meanwhile* ESTELLE *has been plying her powder-puff and lipstick. She looks round for a mirror, fumbles in her bag, then turns towards* GARCIN.]

ESTELLE: Excuse me, have you a glass? [GARCIN *does not answer.*] Any sort of glass, a pocket-mirror will do. [GARCIN *remains silent.*] Even if you won't speak to me, you might lend me a glass.

[*His head still buried in his hands,* GARCIN *ignores her.*]

INEZ [*eagerly*]: Don't worry. I've a glass in my bag. [*She opens her bag. Angrily*] It's gone! They must have taken it from me at the entrance.

ESTELLE: How tiresome!

[*A short silence.* ESTELLE *shuts her eyes and sways, as if about to faint.* INEZ *runs forward and holds her up.*]

INEZ: What's the matter?

ESTELLE [*opens her eyes and smiles*]: I feel so queer. [*She pats herself.*] Don't you ever get taken that way? When I can't see myself I begin to wonder if I really and truly exist. I pat myself just to make sure, but it doesn't help much.

INEZ: You're lucky. I'm always conscious of myself—in my mind. Painfully conscious.

ESTELLE: Ah yes, in your mind. But everything that goes on in one's head is so vague, isn't it? It makes one want to sleep. [*She is silent for a while.*] I've six big mirrors in my bedroom. There they are. I can see them. But they don't see me. They're reflecting the carpet, the settee, the window—but how empty it is, a glass in which I'm absent! When I talked to people I always made sure there was one near by in which I could see myself. I watched myself talking. And somehow it kept me alert, seeing myself as the others saw me. . . . Oh dear! My lipstick! I'm sure I've put it on all crooked. No, I can't do without a looking-glass for ever and ever, I simply can't.

INEZ: Suppose I try to be your glass? Come and pay me a visit, dear. Here's a place for you on my sofa.

ESTELLE: But— [*Points to* GARCIN.]

INEZ: Oh, he doesn't count.

ESTELLE: But we're going to—to hurt each other. You said it yourself.

INEZ: Do I look as if I wanted to hurt you?

◊◊◊

ESTELLE : One never can tell.

INEZ : Much more likely *you'll* hurt *me*. Still, what does it matter ? If I've got to suffer, it may as well be at your hands, your pretty hands. Sit down. Come closer. Closer. Look into my eyes. What do you see ?

ESTELLE : Oh, I'm there ! But so tiny I can't see myself properly.

INEZ : But *I* can. Every inch of you. Now ask me questions. I'll be as candid as any looking-glass.

[ESTELLE *seems rather embarrassed and turns to* GAR-CIN, *as if appealing to him for help.*]

ESTELLE : Please, Mr. Garcin. Sure our chatter isn't boring you ?

[GARCIN *makes no reply.*]

INEZ : Don't worry about him. As I said, he doesn't count. We're by ourselves. . . . Ask away.

ESTELLE : Are my lips all right ?

INEZ : Show ! No, they're a bit smudgy.

ESTELLE : I thought as much. Luckily [*throws a quick glance at* GARCIN] no one's seen me. I'll try again.

INEZ : That's better. No. Follow the line of your lips. Wait ! I'll guide your hand. There. That's quite good.

ESTELLE : As good as when I came in ?

INEZ : Far better. Crueler. Your mouth looks quite diabolical that way.

ESTELLE : Good gracious ! And you say you like it ! How maddening, not being able to see for myself ! You're quite sure, Miss Serrano, that it's all right now ?

INEZ : Won't you call me Inez ?

ESTELLE : Are you sure it looks all right ?

INEZ : You're lovely, Estelle.

ESTELLE : But how can I rely upon your taste ? Is it the same as *my* taste ? Oh, how sickening it all is, enough to drive one crazy !

INEZ : I *have* your taste, my dear, because I like you so much. Look at me. No, straight. Now smile. I'm not so ugly, either. Am I not nicer than your glass ?

ESTELLE : Oh, I don't know. You scare me rather. My reflection in the glass never did that; of course, I knew it so well. Like something I had tamed. . . . I'm going to smile, and my smile will sink down into your pupils, and heaven knows what it will become.

INEZ : And why shouldn't you "tame" *me* ? [*The women gaze at each other,* ESTELLE *with a sort of fearful fascination.*] Listen ! I want you to call me Inez. We must be great friends.

ESTELLE : I don't make friends with women very easily.

INEZ : Not with postal clerks, you mean ? Hullo, what's that—that nasty red spot at the bottom of your cheek ? A pimple ?

ESTELLE : A pimple ? Oh, how simply foul ! Where ?

INEZ : There. . . . You know the way they catch larks—with a mirror ? I'm your lark-mirror, my dear, and you can't escape me. . . . There isn't any pimple, not a trace of one. So what about it ? Suppose the mirror started telling lies ? Or suppose I covered my eyes—as he is doing—and refused to look at you, all that loveliness of yours would be wasted on the desert air. No, don't be afraid, I can't help looking at you, I shan't turn my eyes away. And I'll be nice to you, ever so nice. Only you must be nice to me, too.

[*A short silence.*]

ESTELLE : Are you really—attracted by me ?

INEZ : Very much indeed.

[*Another short silence.*]

ESTELLE [*indicating* GARCIN *by a slight movement of her head*] : But I wish he'd notice me, too.

INEZ : Of course ! Because he's a Man ! [*To* GARCIN] You've won. [GARCIN *says nothing.*] But look at her, damn it ! [*Still no reply from* GARCIN.] Don't pretend. You haven't missed a word of what we've said.

GARCIN : Quite so; not a word. I stuck my fingers in my ears, but your voices thudded in my brain. Silly chatter. Now will you leave me in peace, you two ? I'm not interested in you.

INEZ : Not in me, perhaps—but how about this child ? Aren't you interested in her ? Oh, I saw through your game; you got on your high horse just to impress her.

GARCIN : I asked you to leave me in peace. There's someone talking about me in the newspaper office and I want to listen. And, if it'll make you any happier, let me tell you that I've no use for the "child," as you call her.

ESTELLE : Thanks.

GARCIN : Oh, I didn't mean it rudely.

ESTELLE : You cad !

[*They confront each other in silence for some moments.*]

GARCIN : So that's that. [*Pause.*] You know I begged
you not to speak.

ESTELLE : It's *her* fault; she started. I didn't ask anything of her and she came and offered me her—her
glass.

INEZ : So you say. But all the time you were making up
to him, trying every trick to catch his attention.

ESTELLE : Well, why shouldn't I ?

GARCIN : You're crazy, both of you. Don't you see
where this is leading us ? For pity's sake, keep your
mouths shut. [*Pause.*] Now let's all sit down again
quite quietly; we'll look at the floor and each must
try to forget the others are there.

[*A longish silence.* GARCIN *sits down. The women
return hesitantly to their places. Suddenly* INEZ
swings round on him.]

INEZ : To forget about the others ? How utterly absurd ! I *feel* you there, in every pore. Your silence
clamors in my ears. You can nail up your mouth, cut
your tongue out—but you can't prevent your *being
there.* Can you stop your thoughts ? I hear them
ticking away like a clock, tick-tock, tick-tock, and
I'm certain you hear mine. It's all very well skulking
on your sofa, but you're everywhere, and every
sound comes to me soiled, because you've inter-
cepted it on its way. Why, you've even stolen my
face; you know it and I don't ! And what about her,
about Estelle? You've stolen her from me, too; if she
and I were alone do you suppose she'd treat me as
she does ? No, take your hands from your face, I
won't leave you in peace—that would suit your

book too well. You'd go on sitting there, in a sort of
trance, like a yogi, and even if I didn't see her I'd feel
it in my bones—that she was making every sound,
even the rustle of her dress, for your benefit, throw-
ing you smiles you didn't see. . . . Well, I won't
stand for that, I prefer to choose my hell; I prefer to
look you in the eyes and fight it out face to face.

GARCIN: Have it your own way. I suppose we were
bound to come to this; they knew what they were
about, and we're easy game. If they'd put me in a
room with men—men can keep their mouths shut.
But it's no use wanting the impossible. [*He goes to*
ESTELLE *and lightly fondles her neck.*] So I attract
you, little girl? It seems you were making eyes
at me?

ESTELLE: Don't touch me.

GARCIN: Why not? We might, anyhow, be natural.
. . . Do you know, I used to be mad about women?
And some were fond of me. So we may as well stop
posing, we've nothing to lose. Why trouble about
politeness, and decorum, and the rest of it? We're
between ourselves. And presently we shall be naked
as—as new-born babes.

ESTELLE: Oh, let me be!

GARCIN: As new-born babes. Well, I'd warned you,
anyhow. I asked so little of you, nothing but peace
and a little silence. I'd put my fingers in my ears.
Gomez was spouting away as usual, standing in the
center of the room, with all the pressmen listening.
In their shirt-sleeves. I tried to hear, but it wasn't too
easy. Things on earth move so quickly, you know.

Couldn't you have held your tongues? Now it's over, he's stopped talking, and what he thinks of me has gone back into his head. Well, we've got to see it through somehow. . . . Naked as we were born. So much the better; I want to know whom I have to deal with.

INEZ: You know already. There's nothing more to learn.

GARCIN: You're wrong. So long as each of us hasn't made a clean breast of it—why they've damned him or her—we know nothing. Nothing that counts. You, young lady, you shall begin. Why? Tell us why. If you are frank, if we bring our specters into the open, it may save us from disaster. So—out with it! Why?

ESTELLE: I tell you I haven't a notion. They wouldn't tell me why.

GARCIN: That's so. They wouldn't tell me, either. But I've a pretty good idea. . . . Perhaps you're shy of speaking first? Right. I'll lead off. [*A short silence.*] I'm not a very estimable person.

INEZ: No need to tell us that. We know you were a deserter.

GARCIN: Let that be. It's only a side-issue. I'm here because I treated my wife abominably. That's all. For five years. Naturally, she's suffering still. There she is: the moment I mention her, I see her. It's Gomez who interests me, and it's she I see. Where's Gomez got to? For five years. There! They've given her back my things; she's sitting by the window, with my coat on her knees. The coat with the twelve bullet-holes. The blood's like rust; a brown ring round each hole. It's quite a museum-piece, that coat; scarred with history. And I used to wear it, fancy! . . . Now, can't you shed a tear, my love? Surely you'll squeeze one out—at last? No? You can't manage it? . . . Night after night I came home blind drunk, stinking of wine and women. She'd sat up for me, of course. But she never cried, never uttered a word of reproach. Only her eyes spoke. Big, tragic eyes. I don't regret anything. I must pay the price, but I shan't whine. . . . It's snowing in the street. Won't you cry, confound you? That woman was a born martyr, you know; a victim by vocation.

INEZ [*almost tenderly*]: Why did you hurt her like that?

GARCIN: It was so easy. A word was enough to make her flinch. Like a sensitive-plant. But never, never a reproach. I'm fond of teasing. I watched and waited. But no, not a tear, not a protest. I'd picked her up out of the gutter, you understand. . . . Now she's stroking the coat. Her eyes are shut and she's feeling with her fingers for the bullet-holes. What are you after? What do you expect? I tell you I regret nothing. The truth is, she admired me too much. Does that mean anything to you?

INEZ: No. Nobody admired *me*.

GARCIN: So much the better. So much the better for you. I suppose all this strikes you as very vague. Well, here's something you can get your teeth into. I brought a half-caste girl to stay in our house. My wife slept upstairs; she must have heard—everything. She was an early riser and, as I and the girl stayed in bed late, she served us our morning coffee.

INEZ : You brute!

GARCIN : Yes, a brute, if you like. But a well-beloved brute. [*A far-away look comes to his eyes.*] No, it's nothing. Only Gomez, and he's not talking about *me.* . . . What were you saying? Yes, a brute. Certainly. Else why should I be here? [*To* INEZ] Your turn.

INEZ : Well, I was what some people down there called "a damned bitch." Damned already. So it's no surprise, being here.

GARCIN : Is that all you have to say?

INEZ : No. There was that affair with Florence. A dead men's tale. With three corpses to it. He to start with; then she and I. So there's no one left, I've nothing to worry about; it was a clean sweep. Only that room. I see it now and then. Empty, with the doors locked. . . . No, they've just unlocked them. "To Let." It's to let; there's a notice on the door. That's—too ridiculous.

GARCIN : Three. Three deaths, you said?

INEZ : Three.

GARCIN : One man and two women?

INEZ : Yes.

GARCIN : Well, well. [*A pause.*] Did he kill himself?

INEZ : He? No, he hadn't the guts for that. Still, he'd every reason; we led him a dog's life. As a matter of fact, he was run over by a tram. A silly sort of end. . . . I was living with them; he was my cousin.

◊◊

GARCIN : Was Florence fair ?

INEZ : Fair ? [*Glances at* ESTELLE.] You know, I don't regret a thing; still, I'm not so very keen on telling you the story.

GARCIN : That's all right. . . . So you got sick of him ?

INEZ : Quite gradually. All sorts of little things got on my nerves. For instance, he made a noise when he was drinking—a sort of gurgle. Trifles like that. He was rather pathetic really. Vulnerable. Why are you smiling ?

GARCIN : Because I, anyhow, am *not* vulnerable.

INEZ : Don't be too sure. . . . I crept inside her skin, she saw the world through my eyes. When she left him, I had her on my hands. We shared a bed-sitting-room at the other end of the town.

GARCIN : And then ?

INEZ : Then that tram did its job. I used to remind her every day: "Yes, my pet, we killed him between us." [*A pause.*] I'm rather cruel, really.

GARCIN : So am I.

INEZ : No, you're not cruel. It's something else.

GARCIN : What ?

INEZ : I'll tell you later. When I say I'm cruel, I mean I can't get on without making people suffer. Like a live coal. A live coal in others' hearts. When I'm alone I flicker out. For six months I flamed away in her heart, till there was nothing but a cinder. One night she got up and turned on the gas while I was asleep. Then she crept back into bed. So now you know.

GARCIN : Well ! Well !

◇◇◇

INEZ : Yes ? What's in your mind ?

GARCIN : Nothing. Only that it's not a pretty story.

INEZ : Obviously. But what matter ?

GARCIN : As you say, what matter ? [*To* ESTELLE] Your turn. What have you done ?

ESTELLE : As I told you, I haven't a notion. I rack my brain, but it's no use.

GARCIN : Right. Then we'll give you a hand. That fellow with the smashed face, who was he ?

ESTELLE : Who—who do you mean ?

INEZ : You know quite well. The man you were so scared of seeing when you came in.

ESTELLE : Oh, him ! A friend of mine.

GARCIN : Why were you afraid of him ?

ESTELLE : That's my business, Mr. Garcin.

INEZ : Did he shoot himself on your account ?

ESTELLE : Of course not. How absurd you are !

GARCIN : Then why should you have been so scared ? He blew his brains out, didn't he ? That's how his face got smashed.

ESTELLE : Don't ! Please don't go on.

GARCIN : Because of you. Because of you.

INEZ : He shot himself because of you.

ESTELLE : Leave me alone ! It's—it's not fair, bullying me like that. I want to go ! I want to go !

[*She runs to the door and shakes it.*]

GARCIN : Go if you can. Personally, I ask for nothing better. Unfortunately, the door's locked.

[ESTELLE *presses the bell-push, but the bell does not ring.* INEZ *and* GARCIN *laugh.* ESTELLE *swings round on them, her back to the door.*]

◇◇◇

ESTELLE [*in a muffled voice*] : You're hateful, both of you.

INEZ : Hateful? Yes, that's the word. Now get on with it. That fellow who killed himself on your account —you were his mistress, eh?

GARCIN : Of course she was. And he wanted to have her to himself alone. That's so, isn't it?

INEZ : He danced the tango like a professional, but he was poor as a church mouse—that's right, isn't it? [*A short silence.*]

GARCIN : Was he poor or not? Give a straight answer.

ESTELLE : Yes, he was poor.

GARCIN : And then you had your reputation to keep up. One day he came and implored you to run away with him, and you laughed in his face.

INEZ : That's it. You laughed at him. And so he killed himself.

ESTELLE : Did you use to look at Florence in that way?

INEZ : Yes.

[*A short pause, then* ESTELLE *bursts out laughing.*]

ESTELLE : You've got it all wrong, you two. [*She stiffens her shoulders, still leaning against the door, and faces them. Her voice grows shrill, truculent.*] He wanted me to have a baby. So there!

GARCIN : And you didn't want one?

ESTELLE : I certainly didn't. But the baby came, worse luck. I went to Switzerland for five months. No one knew anything. It was a girl. Roger was with me when she was born. It pleased him no end, having a daughter. It didn't please *me!*

GARCIN : And then?

◇◇◇

ESTELLE : There was a balcony overlooking the lake. I brought a big stone. He could see what I was up to and he kept on shouting : "Estelle, for God's sake, don't !" I hated him then. He saw it all. He was leaning over the balcony and he saw the rings spreading on the water—

GARCIN : Yes ? And then ?

ESTELLE : That's all. I came back to Paris—and he did as he wished.

GARCIN : You mean he blew his brains out ?

ESTELLE : It was absurd of him, really; my husband never suspected anything. [*A pause.*] Oh, how I loathe you ! [*She sobs tearlessly.*]

GARCIN : Nothing doing. Tears don't flow in this place.

ESTELLE : I'm a coward. A coward ! [*Pause.*] If you knew how I hate you !

INEZ [*taking her in her arms*] : Poor child ! [*To GARCIN*] So the hearing's over. But there's no need to look like a hanging judge.

GARCIN : A hanging judge ? [*He glances around him.*] I'd give a lot to be able to see myself in a glass. [*Pause.*] How hot it is ! [*Unthinkingly he takes off his coat.*] Oh, sorry ! [*He starts putting it on again.*]

ESTELLE : Don't bother. You can stay in your shirt-sleeves. As things are—

GARCIN : Just so. [*He drops his coat on the sofa.*] You mustn't be angry with me, Estelle.

ESTELLE : I'm not angry with you.

INEZ : And what about me ? Are you angry with me ?

ESTELLE : Yes.

[*A short silence.*]

◇◇

INEZ : Well, Mr. Garcin, now you have us in the nude all right. Do you understand things any better for that?

GARCIN : I wonder. Yes, perhaps a trifle better. [*Timidly*] And now suppose we start trying to help each other.

INEZ : I don't need help.

GARCIN : Inez, they've laid their snare damned cunningly—like a cobweb. If you make any movement, if you raise your hand to fan yourself, Estelle and I feel a little tug. Alone, none of us can save himself or herself; we're linked together inextricably. So you can take your choice. [*A pause.*] Hullo? What's happening?

INEZ : They've let it. The windows are wide open, a man is sitting on my bed. *My* bed, if you please! They've let it, let it! Step in, step in, make yourself at home, you brute! Ah, there's a woman, too. She's going up to him, putting her hands on his shoulders. . . . Damn it, why don't they turn the lights on? It's getting dark. Now he's going to kiss her. But that's my room, *my* room! Pitch-dark now. I can't see anything, but I hear them whispering, whispering. Is he going to make love to her on *my* bed? What's that she said? That it's noon and the sun is shining? I must be going blind. [*A pause.*] Blacked out. I can't see or hear a thing. So I'm done with the earth, it seems. No more alibis for me! [*She shudders.*] I feel so empty, desiccated—really dead at last. All of me's here, in this room. [*A pause.*] What were you saying? Something about helping me, wasn't it?

GARCIN : Yes.

INEZ : Helping me to do what?

GARCIN : To defeat their devilish tricks.

INEZ : And what do you expect me to do, in return?

GARCIN : To help *me*. It only needs a little effort, Inez; just a spark of human feeling.

INEZ : Human feeling. That's beyond my range. I'm rotten to the core.

GARCIN : And how about me? [*A pause.*] All the same, suppose we try?

INEZ : It's no use. I'm all dried up. I can't give and I can't receive. How could *I* help you? A dead twig, ready for the burning. [*She falls silent, gazing at* ESTELLE, *who has buried her head in her hands.*] Florence was fair, a natural blonde.

GARCIN : Do you realize that this young woman's fated to be your torturer?

INEZ : Perhaps I've guessed it.

GARCIN : It's through her they'll get you. I, of course, I'm different—aloof. I take no notice of her. Suppose you had a try—

INEZ : Yes?

GARCIN : It's a trap. They're watching you, to see if you'll fall into it.

INEZ : I know. And you're another trap. Do you think they haven't foreknown every word you say? And of course there's a whole nest of pitfalls that we can't see. Everything here's a booby-trap. But what do I

◇◇◇

care? I'm a pitfall, too. For her, obviously. And perhaps I'll catch her.

GARCIN: You won't catch anything. We're chasing
after each other, round and round in a vicious circle,
like the horses on a roundabout. That's part of their
plan, of course. . . . Drop it, Inez. Open your
hands and let go of everything. Or else you'll bring
disaster on all three of us.

INEZ: Do I look the sort of person who lets go? I
know what's coming to me. I'm going to burn, and
it's to last forever. Yes, I *know* everything. But do
you think I'll let go? I'll catch her, she'll see you
through my eyes, as Florence saw that other man.
What's the good of trying to enlist my sympathy?
I assure you I know everything, and I can't feel
sorry even for myself. A trap! Don't I know it, and
that I'm in a trap myself, up to the neck, and there's
nothing to be done about it? And if it suits their
book, so much the better!

GARCIN [*gripping her shoulders*]: Well, *I*, anyhow,
can feel sorry for you, too. Look at me, we're naked,
naked right through, and I can see into your heart.
That's one link between us. Do you think I'd want
to hurt you? I don't regret anything, I'm dried up,
too. But for you I can still feel pity.

INEZ [*who has let him keep his hands on her shoulders
until now, shakes herself loose*]: Don't. I hate being
pawed about. And keep your pity for yourself.
Don't forget, Garcin, that there are traps for you,
too, in this room. All nicely set for you. You'd do

better to watch your own interests. [*A pause.*] But, if you will leave us in peace, this child and me, I'll see I don't do you any harm.

GARCIN [*gazes at her for a moment, then shrugs his shoulders*] : Very well.

ESTELLE [*raising her head*] : Please, Garcin.

GARCIN : What do you want of me?

ESTELLE [*rises and goes up to him*] : You can help *me*, anyhow.

GARCIN : If you want help, apply to her.

[INEZ *has come up and is standing behind* ESTELLE, *but without touching her. During the dialogue that follows she speaks almost in her ear. But* ESTELLE *keeps her eyes on* GARCIN, *who observes her without speaking, and she addresses her answers to him, as if it were he who is questioning her.*]

ESTELLE : I implore you, Garcin—you gave me your promise, didn't you? Help me quick. I don't want to be left alone. Olga's taken him to a cabaret.

INEZ : Taken whom?

ESTELLE : Peter. . . . Oh, now they're dancing together.

INEZ : Who's Peter?

ESTELLE : Such a silly boy. He called me his glancing stream—just fancy! He was terribly in love with me. . . . She's persuaded him to come out with her tonight.

INEZ : Do you love him?

ESTELLE : They're sitting down now. She's puffing like a grampus. What a fool the girl is to insist on dancing! But I dare say she does it to reduce. . . . No, of course I don't love him; he's only eighteen, and I'm not a baby-snatcher.

INEZ: Then why bother about them? What difference can it make?

ESTELLE: He belonged to me.

INEZ: Nothing on earth belongs to you any more.

ESTELLE: I tell you he was mine. All mine.

INEZ: Yes, he *was* yours—once. But now— Try to make him hear, try to touch him. Olga can touch him, talk to him as much as she likes. That's so, isn't it? She can squeeze his hands, rub herself against him—

ESTELLE: Yes, look! She's pressing her great fat chest against him, puffing and blowing in his face. But, my poor little lamb, can't you see how ridiculous she is? Why don't you laugh at her? Oh, once I'd have only had to glance at them and she'd have slunk away. Is there really nothing, nothing left of me?

INEZ: Nothing whatever. Nothing of you's left on earth—not even a shadow. All you own is here. Would you like that paper-knife? Or that ornament on the mantelpiece? That blue sofa's yours. And I, my dear, am yours forever.

ESTELLE: You mine! That's good! Well, which of you two would dare to call me his glancing stream, his crystal girl? You know too much about me, you know I'm rotten through and through. . . . Peter dear, think of me, fix your thoughts on me, and save me. All the time you're thinking "my glancing stream, my crystal girl," I'm only half here, I'm only half wicked, and half of me is down there with you, clean and bright and crystal-clear as running water. . . . Oh, just look at her face, all scarlet, like a tomato! No, it's absurd, we've laughed at her together, you and I, often and often. . . . What's that tune? —I always loved it. Yes, the *St. Louis Blues*. . . . All right, dance away, dance away. Garcin, I wish you could see her, you'd die of laughing. Only—she'll never know I *see* her. Yes, I see you, Olga, with your hair all anyhow, and you do look a dope, my dear. Oh, now you're treading on his toes. It's a scream! Hurry up! Quicker! Quicker! He's dragging her along, bundling her round and round—it's too ghastly! He always said I was so light, he loved to dance with me. [*She is dancing as she speaks.*] I tell you, Olga, I can see you. No, she doesn't care, she's dancing through my gaze. What's that? What's that you said? "Our poor dear Estelle"? Oh, don't be such a humbug! You didn't even shed a tear at the funeral. . . . And she has the nerve to talk to him about her poor dear friend Estelle! How dare she discuss me with Peter? Now then, keep time. She never could dance and talk at once. Oh, what's that? No, no. Don't tell him. Please, please don't tell him. You can keep him, do what you like with him, but please don't tell him about—that! [*She has stopped dancing.*] All right. You can have him now. Isn't it *foul*, Garcin? She's told him everything, about Roger, my trip to Switzerland, the baby. "Poor Estelle wasn't exactly—" No, I wasn't exactly— True enough. He's looking grave, shaking his head, but he doesn't seem so very much surprised, not what one would expect. Keep him, then—I won't haggle with you over his long eyelashes, his pretty girlish face. They're yours for the asking. His glancing stream, his crystal. Well, the crystal's shattered into bits. "Poor Estelle!" Dance, dance, dance. On with it. But do keep time. One, two. One, two. How I'd love to go down to earth for just a moment, and dance with him again. [*She dances again for some moments.*] The music's growing fainter. They've turned down the lights, as they do for a tango. Why are they playing so softly? Louder, please. I can't hear. It's so far away, so far away. I—I can't hear a sound. [*She stops dancing.*] All over. It's the end. The earth has left me. [*To* GARCIN] Don't turn from me—please. Take me in your arms. [*Behind* ESTELLE's *back*, INEZ *signs to* GARCIN *to move away.*]

INEZ [*commandingly*] : Now then, Garcin!

[GARCIN *moves back a step, and, glancing at* ESTELLE, *points to* INEZ.]

GARCIN : It's to her you should say that.

ESTELLE [*clinging to him*] : Don't turn away. You're a man, aren't you, and surely I'm not such a fright as all that! Everyone says I've lovely hair and, after all, a man killed himself on my account. You have to look at something, and there's nothing here to see except the sofas and that awful ornament and the table. Surely I'm better to look at than a lot of stupid furniture. Listen! I've dropped out of their hearts like a little sparrow fallen from its nest. So gather me up, dear, fold me to your heart—and you'll see how nice I can be.

GARCIN [*freeing himself from her, after a short struggle*] : I tell you it's to that lady you should speak.

ESTELLE : To her? But she doesn't count, she's a woman.

INEZ : Oh, I don't count? Is that what you think? But, my poor little fallen nestling, you've been sheltering in my heart for ages, though you didn't realize it. Don't be afraid; I'll keep looking at you for ever and ever, without a flutter of my eyelids, and you'll live in my gaze like a mote in a sunbeam.

ESTELLE : A sunbeam indeed! Don't talk such rubbish! You've tried that trick already, and you should know it doesn't work.

INEZ : Estelle! My glancing stream! My crystal!

ESTELLE : *Your* crystal? It's grotesque. Do you think you can fool me with that sort of talk? Everyone knows by now what I did to my baby. The crystal's shattered, but I don't care. I'm just a hollow dummy, all that's left of me is the outside—but it's not for you.

INEZ : Come to me, Estelle. You shall be whatever you like : a glancing stream, a muddy stream. And deep down in my eyes you'll see yourself just as you want to be.

ESTELLE : Oh, leave me in peace. You haven't any eyes. Oh, damn it, isn't there anything I can do to get rid of you? I've an idea. [*She spits in* INEZ's *face.*] There!

INEZ : Garcin, you shall pay for this.

◇◇

[*A pause.* GARCIN *shrugs his shoulders and goes to* ESTELLE.]

GARCIN : So it's a man you need ?

ESTELLE : Not *any* man. You.

GARCIN : No humbug now. Any man would do your business. As I happen to be here, you want me. Right ! [*He grips her shoulders.*] Mind, I'm not your sort at all, really; I'm not a young nincompoop and I don't dance the tango.

ESTELLE : I'll take you as you are. And perhaps I shall change you.

GARCIN : I doubt it. I shan't pay much attention; I've other things to think about.

ESTELLE : What things ?

GARCIN : They wouldn't interest you.

ESTELLE : I'll sit on your sofa and wait for you to take some notice of me. I promise not to bother you at all.

INEZ [*with a shrill laugh*] : That's right, fawn on him, like the silly bitch you are. Grovel and cringe ! And he hasn't even good looks to commend him !

ESTELLE [*to* GARCIN] : Don't listen to her. She has no eyes, no ears. She's—nothing.

GARCIN : I'll give you what I can. It doesn't amount to much. I shan't love you; I know you too well.

ESTELLE : Do you want me, anyhow ?

GARCIN : Yes.

ESTELLE : I ask no more.

GARCIN : In that case— [*He bends over her.*]

INEZ : Estelle ! Garcin ! You must be going crazy. You're not alone. I'm here too.

◇◇

GARCIN : Of course—but what does it matter?

INEZ : Under my eyes? You couldn't—couldn't do it.

ESTELLE : Why not? I often undressed with my maid looking on.

INEZ [*gripping* GARCIN's *arm*] : Let her alone. Don't paw her with your dirty man's hands.

GARCIN [*thrusting her away roughly*] : Take care. I'm no gentleman, and I'd have no compunction about striking a woman.

INEZ : But you promised me; you promised. I'm only asking you to keep your word.

GARCIN : Why should I, considering you were the first to break our agreement?

[INEZ *turns her back on him and retreats to the far end of the room.*]

INEZ : Very well, have it your own way. I'm the weaker party, one against two. But don't forget I'm here, and watching. I shan't take my eyes off you, Garcin; when you're kissing her, you'll feel them boring into you. Yes, have it your own way, make love and get it over. We're in hell; my turn will come.

[*During the following scene she watches them without speaking.*]

GARCIN [*coming back to* ESTELLE *and grasping her shoulders*] : Now then. Your lips. Give me your lips. [*A pause. He bends to kiss her, then abruptly straightens up.*]

ESTELLE [*indignantly*] : Really! [*A pause.*] Didn't I tell you not to pay any attention to her?

◇◇◇

GARCIN: You've got it wrong. [*Short silence.*] It's Gomez; he's back in the press-room. They've shut the windows; it must be winter down there. Six months since I— Well, I warned you I'd be absent-minded sometimes, didn't I? They're shivering, they've kept their coats on. Funny they should feel the cold like that, when I'm feeling so hot. Ah, this time he's talking about me.

ESTELLE: Is it going to last long? [*Short silence.*] You might at least tell me what he's saying.

GARCIN: Nothing. Nothing worth repeating. He's a swine, that's all. [*He listens attentively.*] A god-damned bloody swine. [*He turns to* ESTELLE.] Let's come back to—to ourselves. Are you going to love me?

ESTELLE [*smiling*]: I wonder now!

GARCIN: Will you trust me?

ESTELLE: What a quaint thing to ask! Considering you'll be under my eyes all the time, and I don't think I've much to fear from Inez, so far as you're concerned.

GARCIN: Obviously. [*A pause. He takes his hands off* ESTELLE's *shoulders.*] I was thinking of another kind of trust. [*Listens.*] Talk away, talk away, you swine. I'm not there to defend myself. [*To* ESTELLE] Estelle, you *must* give me your trust.

ESTELLE: Oh, what a nuisance you are! I'm giving you my mouth, my arms, my whole body—and everything could be so simple. . . . My trust! I haven't any to give, I'm afraid, and you're making me terribly embarrassed. You must have something pretty ghastly on your conscience to make such a fuss about my trusting you.

GARCIN: They shot me.

ESTELLE: I know. Because you refused to fight. Well, why shouldn't you?

GARCIN: I—I didn't exactly refuse. [*In a far-away voice*] I must say he talks well, he makes out a good case against me, but he never says what I should have done instead. Should I have gone to the general and said: "General, I decline to fight"? A mug's game; they'd have promptly locked me up. But I wanted to show my colors, my true colors, do you understand? I wasn't going to be silenced. [*To* ESTELLE] So I—I took the train. . . . They caught me at the frontier.

ESTELLE: Where were you trying to go?

GARCIN: To Mexico. I meant to launch a pacifist newspaper down there. [*A short silence.*] Well, why don't you speak?

ESTELLE: What could I say? You acted quite rightly, as you didn't want to fight. [GARCIN *makes a fretful gesture.*] But, darling, how on earth can I guess what you want me to answer?

INEZ: Can't you guess? Well, *I* can. He wants you to tell him that he bolted like a lion. For "bolt" he did, and that's what's biting him.

GARCIN: "Bolted," "went away"—we won't quarrel over words.

ESTELLE: But you *had* to run away. If you'd stayed they'd have sent you to jail, wouldn't they?

GARCIN: Of course. [*A pause.*] Well, Estelle, am I a coward?

◇◇

ESTELLE: How can I say? Don't be so unreasonable, darling. I can't put myself in your skin. You must decide that for yourself.

GARCIN [*wearily*]: I can't decide.

ESTELLE: Anyhow, you must remember. You must have had reasons for acting as you did.

GARCIN: I had.

ESTELLE: Well?

GARCIN: But were they the real reasons?

ESTELLE: You've a twisted mind, that's your trouble. Plaguing yourself over such trifles!

GARCIN: I'd thought it all out, and I wanted to make a stand. But was that my real motive?

INEZ: Exactly. That's the question. Was that your real motive? No doubt you argued it out with yourself, you weighed the pros and cons, you found good reasons for what you did. But fear and hatred and all the dirty little instincts one keeps dark—they're motives too. So carry on, Mr. Garcin, and try to be honest with yourself—for once.

GARCIN: Do I need you to tell me that? Day and night I paced my cell, from the window to the door, from the door to the window. I pried into my heart, I sleuthed myself like a detective. By the end of it I felt as if I'd given my whole life to introspection. But always I harked back to the one thing certain—that I had acted as I did, I'd taken that train to the frontier. But why? Why? Finally I thought: My death will settle it. If I face death courageously, I'll prove I am no coward.

INEZ: And how did you face death?

◇◇

GARCIN : Miserably. Rottenly. [INEZ *laughs.*] Oh, it was only a physical lapse—that might happen to anyone; I'm not ashamed of it. Only everything's been left in suspense, forever. [*To* ESTELLE] Come here, Estelle. Look at me. I want to feel someone looking at me while they're talking about me on earth. . . . I like green eyes.

INEZ : Green eyes! Just hark to him! And you, Estelle, do you like cowards?

ESTELLE : If you knew how little I care! Coward or hero, it's all one—provided he kisses well.

GARCIN : There they are, slumped in their chairs, sucking at their cigars. Bored they look. Half-asleep. They're thinking: "Garcin's a coward." But only vaguely, dreamily. One's got to think of something. "That chap Garcin was a coward." That's what they've decided, those dear friends of mine. In six months' time they'll be saying: "Cowardly as that skunk Garcin." You're lucky, you two; no one on earth is giving you another thought. But I—I'm long in dying.

INEZ : What about your wife, Garcin?

GARCIN : Oh, didn't I tell you? She's dead.

INEZ : Dead?

GARCIN : Yes, she died just now. About two months ago.

INEZ : Of grief?

GARCIN : What else should she die of? So all is for the best, you see; the war's over, my wife's dead, and I've carved out my place in history.

◇◇

[*He gives a choking sob and passes his hand over his face.* ESTELLE *catches his arm.*]

ESTELLE: My poor darling! Look at me. Please look. Touch me. Touch me. [*She takes his hand and puts it on her neck.*] There! Keep your hand there. [GARCIN *makes a fretful movement.*] No, don't move. Why trouble what those men are thinking? They'll die off one by one. Forget them. There's only me, now.

GARCIN: But *they* won't forget *me*, not they! They'll die, but others will come after them to carry on the legend. I've left my fate in their hands.

ESTELLE: You think too much, that's your trouble.

GARCIN: What else is there to do now? I was a man of action once. . . . Oh, if only I could be with them again, for just one day—I'd fling their lie in their teeth. But I'm locked out; they're passing judgment on my life without troubling about me, and they're right, because I'm dead. Dead and done with. [*Laughs.*] A back number.

[*A short pause.*]

ESTELLE [*gently*]: Garcin.

GARCIN: Still there? Now listen! I want you to do me a service. No, don't shrink away. I know it must seem strange to you, having someone asking you for help; you're not used to that. But if you'll make the effort, if you'll only *will* it hard enough, I dare say we can really love each other. Look at it this way. A thousand of them are proclaiming I'm a coward; but what do numbers matter? If there's someone, just one person, to say quite positively I did not run away, that I'm not the sort who runs away, that I'm brave and decent and the rest of it—well, that one person's faith would save me. Will you have that faith in me? Then I shall love you and cherish you for ever. Estelle—will you?

ESTELLE [*laughing*] : Oh, you dear silly man, do you think I could love a coward?

GARCIN : But just now you said—

ESTELLE : I was only teasing you. I like men, my dear, who're real men, with tough skin and strong hands. You haven't a coward's chin, or a coward's mouth, or a coward's voice, or a coward's hair. And it's for your mouth, your hair, your voice, I love you.

GARCIN : Do you mean this? *Really* mean it?

ESTELLE : Shall I swear it?

GARCIN : Then I snap my fingers at them all, those below and those in here. Estelle, we shall climb out of hell. [INEZ *gives a shrill laugh. He breaks off and stares at her.*] What's that?

INEZ [*still laughing*] : But she doesn't mean a word of what she says. How can you be such a simpleton? "Estelle, am I a coward?" As if she cared a damn either way.

ESTELLE : Inez, how dare you? [*To* GARCIN] Don't listen to her. If you want me to have faith in you, you must begin by trusting me.

INEZ : That's right! That's right! Trust away! She wants a man—that far you can trust her—she wants a man's arm round her waist, a man's smell, a man's eyes glowing with desire. And that's all she wants.

She'd assure you you were God Almighty if she thought it would give you pleasure.

GARCIN : Estelle, is this true ? Answer me. Is it true ?

ESTELLE : What do you expect me to say ? Don't you realize how maddening it is to have to answer questions one can't make head or tail of ? [*She stamps her foot.*] You do make things difficult. . . . Anyhow, I'd love you just the same, even if you were a coward. Isn't that enough ?

[*A short pause.*]

GARCIN [*to the two women*] : You disgust me, both of you. [*He goes towards the door.*]

ESTELLE : What are you up to ?

GARCIN : I'm going.

INEZ [*quickly*] : You won't get far. The door is locked.

GARCIN : I'll *make* them open it. [*He presses the bell-push. The bell does not ring.*]

ESTELLE : Please ! Please !

INEZ [*to* ESTELLE] : Don't worry, my pet. The bell doesn't work.

GARCIN : I tell you they shall open. [*Drums on the door.*] I can't endure it any longer, I'm through with you both. [ESTELLE *runs to him; he pushes her away.*] Go away. You're even fouler than she. I won't let myself get bogged in your eyes. You're soft and slimy. Ugh ! [*Bangs on the door again.*] Like an octopus. Like a quagmire.

ESTELLE : I beg you, oh, I beg you not to leave me. I'll promise not to speak again, I won't trouble you in any way—but don't go. I daren't be left alone with Inez, now she's shown her claws.

◇◇

GARCIN: Look after yourself. I never asked you to come here.

ESTELLE: Oh, how mean you are! Yes, it's quite true you're a coward.

INEZ [*going up to* ESTELLE]: Well, my little sparrow fallen from the nest, I hope you're satisfied now. You spat in my face—playing up to him, of course—and we had a tiff on his account. But he's going, and a good riddance it will be. We two women will have the place to ourselves.

ESTELLE: You won't gain anything. If that door opens, I'm going, too.

INEZ: Where?

ESTELLE: I don't care where. As far from you as I can. [GARCIN *has been drumming on the door while they talk.*]

GARCIN: Open the door! Open, blast you! I'll endure anything, your red-hot tongs and molten lead, your racks and prongs and garrotes—all your fiendish gadgets, everything that burns and flays and tears— I'll put up with any torture you impose. Anything, anything would be better than this agony of mind, this creeping pain that gnaws and fumbles and caresses one and never hurts quite enough. [*He grips the door-knob and rattles it.*] Now will you open? [*The door flies open with a jerk, nearly falling on the floor.*] Ah! [*A long silence.*]

INEZ: Well, Garcin? You're free to go.

GARCIN: [*meditatively*]: Now I wonder why that door opened.

◇◇

INEZ : What are you waiting for? Hurry up and go.

GARCIN : I shall not go.

INEZ : And you, Estelle? [ESTELLE *does not move.* INEZ *bursts out laughing.*] So what? Which shall it be? Which of the three of us will leave? The barrier's down, why are we waiting? . . . But what a situation! It's a scream! We're—inseparables!

[ESTELLE *springs at her from behind.*]

ESTELLE : Inseparables? Garcin, come and lend a hand. Quickly. We'll push her out and slam the door on her. That'll teach her a lesson.

INEZ [*struggling with* ESTELLE] : Estelle! I beg you, let me stay. I won't go, I won't go! Not into the passage.

GARCIN : Let go of her.

ESTELLE : You're crazy. She hates you.

GARCIN : It's because of her I'm staying here.

[ESTELLE *releases* INEZ *and stares dumbfoundedly at* GARCIN.]

INEZ : Because of me? [*Pause.*] All right, shut the door. It's ten times hotter here since it opened. [GARCIN *goes to the door and shuts it.*] Because of me, you said?

GARCIN : Yes. *You,* anyhow, know what it means to be a coward.

INEZ : Yes, I know.

GARCIN : And you know what wickedness is, and shame, and fear. There were days when you peered into yourself, into the secret places of your heart, and what you saw there made you faint with horror.

And then, next day, you didn't know what to make of it, you couldn't interpret the horror you had glimpsed the day before. Yes, you know what evil *costs*. And when you say I'm a coward, you know from experience what that means. Is that so?

INEZ: Yes.

GARCIN: So it's you whom I have to convince; you are of my kind. Did you suppose I meant to go? No, I couldn't leave you here, gloating over my defeat, with all those thoughts about me running in your head.

INEZ: Do you really wish to convince me?

GARCIN: That's the one and only thing I wish for now. I can't hear them any longer, you know. Probably that means they're through with me. For good and all. The curtain's down, nothing of me is left on earth—not even the name of coward. So, Inez, we're alone. Only you two remain to give a thought to me. She—she doesn't count. It's you who matter; you who hate me. If you'll have faith in me I'm saved.

INEZ: It won't be easy. Have a look at me. I'm a hard-headed woman.

GARCIN: I'll give you all the time that's needed.

INEZ: Yes, we've lots of time in hand. *All* time.

GARCIN [*putting his hands on her shoulders*]: Listen! Each man has an aim in life, a leading motive; that's so, isn't it? Well, I didn't give a damn for wealth, or for love. I aimed at being a real man. A tough, as they say. I staked everything on the same horse. . . . Can one possibly be a coward when one's deliberately courted danger at every turn? And can one judge a life by a single action?

INEZ: Why not? For thirty years you dreamt you were a hero, and condoned a thousand petty lapses —because a hero, of course, can do no wrong. An easy method, obviously. Then a day came when you were up against it, the red light of real danger—and you took the train to Mexico.

GARCIN: I "dreamt," you say. It was no dream. When I chose the hardest path, I made my choice deliberately. A man is what he wills himself to be.

INEZ: Prove it. Prove it was no dream. It's what one does, and nothing else, that shows the stuff one's made of.

GARCIN: I died too soon. I wasn't allowed time to—to do my deeds.

INEZ: One always dies too soon—or too late. And yet one's whole life is complete at that moment, with a line drawn neatly under it, ready for the summing up. You are—your life, and nothing else.

GARCIN: What a poisonous woman you are! With an answer for everything.

INEZ: Now then! Don't lose heart. It shouldn't be so hard, convincing me. Pull yourself together, man, rake up some arguments. [GARCIN *shrugs his shoulders.*] Ah, wasn't I right when I said you were vulnerable? Now you're going to pay the price, and what a price! You're a coward, Garcin, because I wish it. I wish it—do you hear?—I wish it. And yet, just look at me, see how weak I am, a mere breath on the air, a gaze observing you, a formless thought that thinks you. [*He walks towards her, opening his hands.*] Ah, they're open now, those big hands, those coarse, man's hands! But what do you hope to do? You can't throttle thoughts with hands. So you've no choice, you must convince me, and you're at my mercy.

ESTELLE: Garcin!

GARCIN: What?

ESTELLE: Revenge yourself.

GARCIN: How?

ESTELLE: Kiss me, darling—then you'll hear her squeal.

GARCIN: That's true, Inez. I'm at your mercy, but you're at mine as well.

[*He bends over* ESTELLE. INEZ *gives a little cry.*]

INEZ: Oh, you coward, you weakling, running to women to console you!

ESTELLE: That's right, Inez. Squeal away.

INEZ: What a lovely pair you make! If you could see his big paw splayed out on your back, rucking up your skin and creasing the silk. Be careful, though! He's perspiring, his hand will leave a blue stain on your dress.

ESTELLE: Squeal away, Inez, squeal away! . . . Hug me tight, darling; tighter still—that'll finish her off, and a good thing too!

INEZ: Yes, Garcin, she's right. Carry on with it, press her to you till you feel your bodies melting into each other; a lump of warm, throbbing flesh. . . . Love's a grand solace, isn't it, my friend? Deep and dark as sleep. But I'll see you don't sleep.

[GARCIN *makes a slight movement.*]

◇◇◇

ESTELLE: Don't listen to her. Press your lips to my mouth. Oh, I'm yours, yours, yours.

INEZ: Well, what are you waiting for? Do as you're told. What a lovely scene: coward Garcin holding baby-killer Estelle in his manly arms! Make your stakes, everyone. Will coward Garcin kiss the lady, or won't he dare? What's the betting? I'm watching you, everybody's watching, I'm a crowd all by myself. Do you hear the crowd? Do you hear them muttering, Garcin? Mumbling and muttering. "Coward! Coward! Coward! Coward!"—that's what they're saying. . . . It's no use trying to escape, I'll never let you go. What do you hope to get from her silly lips? Forgetfulness? But I shan't forget you, not I! "It's I you must convince." So come to me. I'm waiting. Come along, now. . . . Look how obedient he is, like a well-trained dog who comes when his mistress calls. You can't hold him, and you never will.

GARCIN: Will night never come?

INEZ: Never.

GARCIN: You will always see me?

INEZ: Always.

[GARCIN *moves away from* ESTELLE *and takes some steps across the room. He goes to the bronze ornament.*]

GARCIN: This bronze. [*Strokes it thoughtfully.*] Yes, now's the moment; I'm looking at this thing on the mantelpiece, and I understand that I'm in hell. I tell you, everything's been thought out beforehand. They knew I'd stand at the fireplace stroking this thing of bronze, with all those eyes intent on me. Devouring me. [*He swings round abruptly.*] What? Only two of you? I thought there were more; many more. [*Laughs.*] So this is hell. I'd never have believed it. You remember all we were told about the torture-chambers, the fire and brimstone, the "burning marl." Old wives' tales! There's no need for redhot pokers. Hell is—other people!

ESTELLE: My darling! Please—

GARCIN [*thrusting her away*]: No, let me be. She is between us: I cannot love you when she's watching.

ESTELLE: Right! In that case, I'll stop her watching. [*She picks up the paper-knife from the table, rushes at* INEZ, *and stabs her several times.*]

INEZ [*struggling and laughing*]: But, you crazy creature, what do you think you're doing? You know quite well I'm dead.

ESTELLE: Dead?

[*She drops the knife. A pause.* INEZ *picks up the knife and jabs herself with it regretfully.*]

INEZ: Dead! Dead! Dead! Knives, poison, ropes—all useless. It has happened *already*, do you understand? Once and for all. So here we are, forever. [*Laughs.*]

ESTELLE [*with a peal of laughter*]: Forever. My God, how funny! Forever.

GARCIN [*looks at the two women, and joins in the laughter*]: For ever, and ever, and ever.

[*They slump onto their respective sofas. A long silence. Their laughter dies away and they gaze at each other.*]

GARCIN: Well, well, let's get on with it. . . .

CURTAIN

THE FLIES

(*Les Mouches*)

◇◇

A PLAY IN THREE ACTS

CHARACTERS IN THE PLAY

ZEUS

ORESTES

ELECTRA

ÆGISTHEUS

CLYTEMNESTRA

THE TUTOR

FIRST FURY

SECOND FURY

THE HIGH PRIEST

A YOUNG WOMAN

AN OLD WOMAN

AN IDIOT BOY

FIRST SOLDIER

SECOND SOLDIER

MEN AND WOMEN, TOWNSFOLK OF ARGOS

FURIES, SERVANTS, PALACE GUARDS

Les Mouches (*The Flies*) was first played at the Théâtre de la Cité, Paris, under the direction of Charles Dullin

◇◇◇◇◇◇◇◇◇◇◇◇◇◇◇◇◇◇◇◇◇◇◇◇◇◇◇◇◇◇◇

THE FLIES

◇◇◇◇◇◇◇◇◇◇◇◇◇◇◇◇◇◇◇◇◇◇◇◇◇◇◇◇◇◇◇

ACT I

A public square in Argos, dominated by a statue of Zeus, god of flies and death. The image has white eyes and blood-smeared cheeks.

A procession of OLD WOMEN *in black, carrying urns, advances; they make libations to the statue. An* IDIOT BOY *is squatting in the background.* ORESTES *enters, accompanied by* THE TUTOR.

ORESTES: Listen, my good women.
[*The* OLD WOMEN *swing round, emitting little squeals.*]
THE TUTOR: Would you kindly tell us— [*The* OLD WOMEN *spit on the ground and move back a pace.*] Steady, good ladies, steady. I only want a piece of simple information. We are travelers and we have lost our way. [*Dropping their urns, the* WOMEN *take to their heels.*] Stupid old hags! You'd think I had intentions on their virtue! [*Ironically*] Ah, young master, truly this has been a pleasant journey. And how well inspired you were to come to this

city of Argos, when there are hundreds of towns in Greece and Italy where the drink is good, the inns are hospitable, and the streets full of friendly, smiling people! But these uncouth hillmen—one would suppose they'd never seen a foreigner before. A hundred times and more I've had to ask our way, and never once did I get a straight answer. And then the grilling heat! This Argos is a nightmare city. Squeals of terror everywhere, people who panic the moment they set eyes on you, and scurry to cover, like black beetles, down the glaring streets. Pfoo! I can't think how you bear it—this emptiness, the shimmering air, that fierce sun overhead. What's deadlier than the sun?

ORESTES: I was born here.

THE TUTOR: So the story goes. But, if I were you, I wouldn't brag about it.

ORESTES: I was born here—and yet I have to ask my way, like any stranger. Knock at that door.

THE TUTOR: What do you expect? That someone will open it? Only look at those houses and tell me how they strike you. You will observe there's not a window anywhere. They open on closed courtyards, I suppose, and turn their backsides to the street. [ORESTES *makes a fretful gesture.*] Very good, sir. I'll knock—but nothing will come of it.

[*He knocks. Nothing happens. He knocks again, and the door opens a cautious inch.*]

A VOICE: What do you want?

THE TUTOR: Just a word of information. Can you tell me where—? [*The door is slammed in his face.*]

Oh, the devil take you! Well, my lord Orestes, is
that enough, or must I try elsewhere? If you wish,
I'll knock at every door.

ORESTES: No, that's enough.

THE TUTOR: Well, I never! There's someone here.
[*He goes up to the* IDIOT BOY.] Excuse me, sir . . .

THE IDIOT: Hoo! Hoo! Hoo!

THE TUTOR [*bowing again*]: My noble lord . . .

THE IDIOT: Hoo!

THE TUTOR: Will Your Highness deign to show us
where Ægistheus lives?

THE IDIOT: Hoo!

THE TUTOR: Ægistheus, King of Argos.

THE IDIOT: Hoo! Hoo! Hoo!

[ZEUS *passes by, back stage.*]

THE TUTOR: We're out of luck. The only one who
doesn't run away is a half-wit. [ZEUS *retraces his
steps.*] Ah, that's odd! He's followed us here.

ORESTES: Who?

THE TUTOR: That bearded fellow.

ORESTES: You're dreaming.

THE TUTOR: I tell you, I saw him go by.

ORESTES: You must be mistaken.

THE TUTOR: Impossible. Never in my life have I seen
such a beard—or, rather, only one: the bronze
beard on the chin of Zeus Ahenobarbos at Palermo.
Look, there he is again. What can he want of us?

ORESTES: He is only a traveler like ourselves.

THE TUTOR: Only that? We met him on the road to
Delphi. And when we took the boat at Itea, there
he was, fanning that great beard in the bows. At

◇◇◇

Nauplia we couldn't move a step without having him at our heels, and now—here he is again! Do you think that chance explains it? [*He brushes the flies off his face.*] These flies in Argos are much more sociable than its townsfolk Just look at them! [*Points to the* IDIOT BOY.] There must be a round dozen pumping away at each of his eyes, and yet he's smiling quite contentedly; probably he likes having his eyes sucked. That's not surprising; look at that yellow muck oozing out of them. [*He flaps his hand at the flies.*] Move on, my little friends. Hah! They're on you now. Allow me! [*He drives them away.*] Well, this should please you—you who are always complaining of being a stranger in your native land. These charming insects, anyhow, are making you welcome; one would think they know who you are. [*He whisks them away.*] Now leave us in peace, you buzzers. We know you like us, but we've had enough of you. . . . Where can they come from? They're as big as bumble-bees and noisy as a swarm of locusts.

[*Meanwhile* ZEUS *has approached them.*]

ZEUS: They are only bluebottles, a trifle larger than usual. Fifteen years ago a mighty stench of carrion drew them to this city, and since then they've been getting fatter and fatter. Give them another fifteen years, and they'll be as big as toads.

[*A short silence.*]

THE TUTOR: Pray, whom have I the honor of addressing?

ZEUS: Demetrios is my name, and I hail from Athens.

ORESTES: Did I not see you on the boat, a fortnight ago?

ZEUS: Yes, and I saw you, too.

[*Hideous shrieks come from the palace.*]

THE TUTOR: Listen to that! I don't know if you will agree with me, young master, but I think we'd do better to leave this place.

ORESTES: Keep quiet!

ZEUS: You have nothing to fear. It's what they call Dead Men's Day today. Those cries announce the beginning of the ceremony.

ORESTES: You seem well posted on the local customs.

ZEUS: Yes, I often visit Argos. As it so happened, I was here on the great day of Agamemnon's homecoming, when the Greek fleet, flushed with victory, anchored in the Nauplia roads. From the top of the rampart one saw the bay dappled with their white sails. [*He drives the flies away.*] There were no flies then. Argos was only a small country town, basking in the sun, yawning the years away. Like everyone else I went up to the sentry-path to see the royal procession, and I watched it for many an hour wending across the plain. At sundown on the second day Queen Clytemnestra came to the ramparts, and with her was Ægistheus, the present King. The people of Argos saw their faces dyed red by the sunset, and they saw them leaning over the battlements, gazing for a long while seawards. And the people thought: "There's evil brewing." But they kept silence. Ægistheus, you should know, was the Queen's lover. A hard, brutal man, and even in those days he had the

◇◇◇

cast of melancholy. . . . But you're looking pale, young sir.

ORESTES: It's the long journey I have made, and this accursed heat. But pray go on; you interest me.

ZEUS: Agamemnon was a worthy man, you know, but he made one great mistake. He put a ban on public executions. That was a pity. A good hanging now and then—that entertains folk in the provinces and robs death of its glamour. . . . So the people here held their tongues; they looked forward to seeing, for once, a violent death. They still kept silent when they saw their King entering by the city gates. And when Clytemnestra stretched forth her graceful arms, fragrant and white as lilies, they still said nothing. Yet at that moment a word, a single word, might have sufficed. But no one said it; each was gloating in imagination over the picture of a huge corpse with a shattered face.

ORESTES: And you, too, said nothing?

ZEUS: Does that rouse your indignation? Well, my young friend, I like you all the better for it; it proves your heart's in the right place. No, I admit I, too, held my peace. I'm a stranger here, and it was no concern of mine. And next day when it started, when the folk of Argos heard their King screaming his life out in the palace, they still kept silence, but they rolled their eyes in a sort of ecstasy, and the whole town was like a woman in heat.

ORESTES: So now the murderer is on the throne. For fifteen years he has enjoyed the fruits of crime. And I thought the gods were just!

ZEUS: Steady, my friend. Don't blame the gods too hastily. Must they always punish? Wouldn't it be better to use such breaches of the law to point a moral?

ORESTES: And is this what they did?

ZEUS: They sent the flies.

THE TUTOR: The flies? How do the flies come in?

ZEUS: They are a symbol. But if you want to know what the gods did, look around you. See that old creature over there, creeping away like a beetle on her little black feet, and hugging the walls. Well, she's a good specimen of the squat black vermin that teem in every cranny of this town. Now watch me catch our specimen, it's well worth inspection. Here it is. A loathsome object, you'll agree. . . . Hah! You're blinking now. Still, you're an Argive and you should be used to the white-hot rapiers of the sun. . . . Watch her wriggling, like a hooked fish! . . . Now, old lady, let's hear your tale of woe. I see you're in black from head to foot. In mourning for a whole regiment of sons, is that it? Tell us, and I'll release you—perhaps. For whom are you in mourning?

OLD WOMAN: Sir, I am not in mourning. Everyone wears black at Argos.

ZEUS: Everyone wears black? Ah, I see. You're in mourning for your murdered King.

OLD WOMAN: Whisht! For God's sake, don't talk of that.

ZEUS: Yes, you're quite old enough to have heard those huge cries that echoed and re-echoed for a whole morning in the city streets. What did you do about it?

OLD WOMAN: My good man was in the fields, at work. What could I do, a woman alone? I bolted my door.

ZEUS: Yes, but you left your window not quite closed, so as to hear the better, and, while you peeped behind the curtains and held your breath, you felt a little tingling itch between your loins, and didn't you enjoy it!

OLD WOMAN: Oh, please stop, sir!

ZEUS: And when you went to bed that night, you had a grand time with your man. A real gala night.

OLD WOMAN: A what? . . . No, my lord, that was a dreadful, dreadful night.

ZEUS: A red gala, I tell you, and you've never been able to blot out its memory.

OLD WOMAN: Mercy on us! Are you—are you one of the Dead?

ZEUS: I dead? You're crazy, woman. . . . Anyhow, don't trouble your head who I am; you'd do better to think of yourself, and try to earn forgiveness by repenting of your sins.

OLD WOMAN: Oh, sir, I do repent, most heartily I repent. If you only knew how I repent, and my daughter too, and my son-in-law offers up a heifer every year, and my little grandson has been brought up in a spirit of repentance. He's a pretty lad, with flaxen hair, and he always behaves as good as gold. Though he's only seven, he never plays or laughs, for thinking of his original sin.

ZEUS: Good, you old bitch, that's as it should be—and

be sure you die in a nice bitchy odor of repentance.
It's your one hope of salvation. [*The* OLD WOMAN
runs away.] Unless I'm much mistaken, my masters,
we have there the real thing, the good old piety of
yore, rooted in terror.

ORESTES: What man are you?

ZEUS: Who cares what I am? We were talking of the
gods. Well now, should they have struck Ægistheus
down?

ORESTES: They should. . . . They should. . . . Oh,
how would I know what they should have done?
What do I care, anyhow? I'm a stranger here. . . .
Does Ægistheus feel contrition?

ZEUS: Ægistheus? I'd be much surprised. But what
matter? A whole city's repenting on his account.
And it's measured by the bushel, is repentance.
[*Eerie screams in the palace*.] Listen! Lest they forget the screams of the late King in his last agony,
they keep this festival of death each year when the
day of the King's murder comes round. A herdsman
from the hills—he's chosen for his lung-power—is
set to bellow in the Great Hall of the palace. [ORES-
TES *makes a gesture of disgust*.] Bah! That's nothing. I wonder what you'll say presently, when they
let the Dead loose. Fifteen years ago, to a day,
Agamemnon was murdered. And what a change has
come over the light-hearted folk of Argos since that
day; how near and dear to me they are at present!

ORESTES: Dear to *you*?

ZEUS: Pay no heed, young man. That was a slip of the
tongue. Near and dear to the gods, I meant.

ORESTES: You surprise me. Then those blood-smeared walls, these swarms of flies, this reek of shambles and the stifling heat, these empty streets and yonder god with his gashed face, and all those creeping, half-human creatures beating their breasts in darkened rooms, and those shrieks, those hideous, blood-curdling shrieks—can it be that Zeus and his Olympians delight in these?

ZEUS: Young man, do not sit in judgment on the gods. They have their secrets—and their sorrows.

[*A short silence.*]

ORESTES: Am I right in thinking Agamemnon had a daughter? A daughter named Electra?

ZEUS: Yes. She lives there, in the palace—that building yonder.

ORESTES: So that's the palace? . . . And what does Electra think of—all this?

ZEUS: Oh, she's a mere child. There was a son, too, named Orestes. But he's dead, it seems.

ORESTES: Dead? Well, really . . .

THE TUTOR: Of course he's dead, young master. I thought you knew it. Don't you remember what they told us at Nauplia—about Ægistheus' having him murdered, soon after Agamemnon's death?

ZEUS: Still, some say he's alive. The story goes that the men ordered to kill the child had pity on him and left him in the forest. Some rich Athenians found him there and took him home. For my part, I'd rather he were dead.

ORESTES: Pray, why?

ZEUS: Suppose that one day he appeared in this city, and—

ORESTES: Continue, please.

ZEUS: As you wish. . . . Well, I'd say this to him. "My lad—" I'd say, "My lad," as he's your age or thereabouts—if he's alive, of course. By the way, young lord, may I know your name?

ORESTES: Philebus is my name, and I hail from Corinth. I am traveling to improve my mind, and this old slave accompanying me used to be my tutor.

ZEUS: Thank you. Well, I'd say something like this. "My lad, get you gone! What business have you here? Do you wish to enforce your rights? Yes, you're brave and strong and spirited. I can see you as a captain in an army of good fighters. You have better things to do than reigning over a dead-and-alive city, a carrion city plagued by flies. These people are great sinners but, as you see, they're working out their atonement. Let them be, young fellow, let them be; respect their sorrowful endeavor, and begone on tiptoe. You cannot share in their repentance, since you did not share their crime. Your brazen innocence makes a gulf between you and them. So if you have any care for them, be off! Be off, or you will work their doom. If you hinder them on their way, if even for a moment you turn their thoughts from their remorse, all their sins will harden on them—like cold fat. They have guilty consciences, they're afraid—and fear and guilty consciences have a good savor in the nostrils of the gods. Yes, the gods take pleasure in such poor souls. Would you oust them from the favor of the gods? What, moreover, could you give them in exchange? Good digestions, the gray monotony of provincial life, and the boredom—ah, the soul-destroying boredom—of long days of mild content. Go your way, my lad, go your way. The repose of cities and men's souls hangs on a thread; tamper with it and you bring disaster. [*Looking him in the eyes*] A disaster which will recoil on you."

ORESTES: Yes? So that is what you'd say? Well, if I were that young man, I'd answer— [*They eye each other truculently.* THE TUTOR *coughs.*] No, I don't know how I'd answer you. Perhaps you're right, and anyhow it's no concern of mine.

ZEUS: Good. I only hope Orestes would show as much sense. . . . Well, peace be with you, my friend; I must go about my business.

ORESTES: Peace be with you.

ZEUS: By the way, if those flies bother you, here's a way of getting rid of them. You see that swarm buzzing round your head? Right. Now watch! I flick my wrist—so—and wave my arm once, and then I say: Abraxas, galla, galla, tsay, tsay. See! They're falling down and starting to crawl on the ground like caterpillars.

ORESTES: By Jove!

ZEUS: Oh, that's nothing. Just a parlor trick. I'm a fly-charmer in my leisure hours. Good day to you. We shall meet again.

[*Exit* ZEUS.]

THE TUTOR : Take care. That man knows who you are.

ORESTES : "Man," you say. But *is* he a man?

THE TUTOR : What else should he be? You grieve me, my young master. Have all my lessons, all my precepts, the smiling skepticism I taught you, been wasted on your ears? "Is he a man?" you ask. There's nothing else but men—what more would you have? And that bearded fellow is a man, sure enough; probably one of Ægistheus' spies.

ORESTES : A truce to your philosophy! It's done me too much harm already.

THE TUTOR : Harm? Do you call it doing harm to people when one emancipates their minds? Ah, how you've changed! Once I read you like an open book. . . . But at least you might tell me your plans. Why bring me to this city, and what's your purpose here?

ORESTES : Did I say I had a purpose? But that's enough. Be silent now. [*He takes some steps towards the palace.*] That is *my* palace. My father's birthplace. And it's there a whore and her paramour foully butchered him. I, too, was born there. I was nearly three when that usurper's bravoes carried me away. Most likely we went out by that door. One of them held me in his arms, I had my eyes wide open, and no doubt I was crying. And yet I have no memories, none whatever. I am looking at a huge, gloomy building, solemn and pretentious in the worst provincial taste. I am looking at it, but I *see* it for the first time.

THE TUTOR : No memories, master? What ingratitude, considering that I gave ten years of my life to stock-

◇◇

ing you with them! And what of all the journeys we have made together, all the towns we visited? And the course in archæology I composed specially for you? No memories, indeed! Palaces, shrines, and temples—with so many of them is your memory peopled that you could write a guide-book of all Greece.

ORESTES: Palaces—that's so. Palaces, statues, pillars—stones, stones, stones! Why, with all those stones in my head, am I not heavier? While you are about it, why not remind me of the three hundred and eighty-seven steps of the temple at Ephesus? I climbed them, one by one, and I remember each. The seventeenth, if my memory serves me, was badly broken. And yet—! Why, an old, mangy dog, warming himself at the hearth, and struggling to his feet with a little whimper to welcome his master home—why, that dog has more memories than I! At least he recognizes his master. *His* master. But what can I call mine?

THE TUTOR: And what of your culture, Lord Orestes? What of that? All that wise lore I culled for you with loving care, like a bouquet, matching the fruits of my knowledge with the finest flowers of my experience? Did I not, from the very first, set you a-reading all the books there are, so as to make clear to you the infinite diversity of men's opinions? And did I not remind you, time and again, how variable are human creeds and customs? So, along with youth, good looks, and wealth, you have the wisdom of far riper years; your mind is free from prejudice and superstition; you have no family ties, no religion, and no calling; you are free to turn your hand to anything. But you know better than to commit yourself—and there lies your strength. So, in a word, you stand head and shoulders above the ruck and, what's more, you could hold a chair of philosophy or architecture in a great university. And yet you cavil at your lot!

ORESTES: No, I do not cavil. What should I cavil at? You've left me free as the strands torn by the wind from spiders' webs that one sees floating ten feet above the ground. I'm light as gossamer and walk on air. I know I'm favored, I appreciate my lot at its full value. [*A pause.*] Some men are born bespoken; a certain path has been assigned them, and at its end there is something they *must* do, a deed allotted. So on and on they trudge, wounding their bare feet on the flints. I suppose that strikes *you* as vulgar—the joy of going somewhere definite. And there are others, men of few words, who bear deep down in their hearts a load of dark imaginings; men whose whole life was changed because one day in childhood, at the age of five or seven— Right; I grant you these are no great men. When I was seven, I know I had no home, no roots. I let sounds and scents, the patter of rain on housetops, the golden play of sunbeams, slip past my body and fall round me—and I knew these were for others, I could never make them *my* memories. For memories are luxuries reserved for people who own houses, cattle, fields and servants. Whereas I—! I'm free as air, thank God. My mind's

◇◇◇

my own, gloriously aloof. [*He goes nearer to the palace.*] I might have lived there. I'd not have read any of your books; perhaps I'd not have learned to read. It's rare for a Greek prince to know how to read. But I'd have come in and gone out by that door ten thousand times. As a child I'd have played with its leaves, and when I pushed at them with all my little might, they'd have creaked without yielding, and I'd have taken the measure of my weakness. Later on, I'd have pushed them open furtively by night and gone out after girls. And some years later, when I came of age, the slaves would have flung the doors wide open and I'd have crossed the threshold on horseback. My old wooden door! I'd have been able to find your keyhole with my eyes shut. And that notch there—I might have made it showing off, the first day they let me hold a spear. [*He steps back.*] Let's see. That's the Dorian style, isn't it? And what do you make of that gold inlay? I saw the like at Dodona; a pretty piece of craftsmanship. And now I'm going to say something that will rejoice you. This is not *my* palace, nor *my* door. And there's nothing to detain us here.

THE TUTOR: Ah, that's talking sense. For what would you have gained by living in Argos? By now your spirit would be broken, you'd be wallowing in repentance.

ORESTES: Still, it would be *my* repentance. And this furnace heat singeing my hair would be *mine*. Mine, too, the buzz of all these flies. At this moment I'd be lying naked in some dark room at the back of the

◇◇◇

palace, and watching a ribbon of red light lengthen across the floor. I'd be waiting for sundown; waiting for the cool dusk of an Argos evening to rise like perfume from the parched earth; an Argos evening like many a thousand others, familiar yet ever new, another evening that should be *mine*. . . . Well, well, my worthy pedagogue, let's be off. We've no business to be luxuriating in others' heat.

THE TUTOR : Ah, my young lord, how you've eased my mind! During these last few months—to be exact, ever since I revealed to you the secret of your birth —I could see you changing day by day, and it gave me many a sleepless night. I was afraid—

ORESTES : Of what?

THE TUTOR : No, it will anger you.

ORESTES : Speak.

THE TUTOR : Be it so. Well, though from one's earliest years one has been trained to skeptic irony, one can't help having foolish fancies now and then. And I wondered if you weren't hatching some wild scheme to oust Ægistheus and take his place.

ORESTES [*thoughtfully*] : To oust Ægistheus. Ah— [*A pause.*] No, my good slave, you need not fear; the time for that is past. True, nothing could please me better than to grip that sanctimonious ruffian by the beard and drag him from my father's throne. But what purpose would it serve? These folk are no concern of mine. I have not seen one of their children come into the world, nor been present at their daughters' weddings; I don't share their remorse, I don't even know a single one of them by name. That bearded fellow was right; a king should share his subjects' memories. So we'll let them be, and begone on tiptoe. . . . But, mind you, if there were something I could do, something to give me the freedom of the city; if, even by a crime, I could acquire their memories, their hopes and fears, and fill with these the void within me, yes, even if I had to kill my own mother—

THE TUTOR: Hush! For heaven's sake, hush!

ORESTES: Yes, these are idle dreams. Let's be off. Now go and see if we can get some horses here, and we'll move on to Sparta, where I have good friends.

[ELECTRA *comes forward, carrying a large ash-can. She goes up to the statue of* ZEUS, *without seeing them.*]

ELECTRA: Yes, you old swine, scowl away at me with your goggle eyes and your fat face all smeared with raspberry juice—scowl away, but you won't scare me, not you! They've been to worship you, haven't they?—those pious matrons in black dresses. They've been padding round you in their big creaky shoes. And you were pleased, old bugaboo, it warmed your silly wooden heart. You like them old, of course; the nearer they're to corpses, the more you love them. They've poured their choicest wines out at your feet, because it's your festival today, and the stale smell from their petticoats tickled your nostrils. [*She rubs herself against him.*] Now smell me for a change, smell the perfume of a fresh, clean body. But, of course, I'm young, I'm alive—and you loathe youth and life. I, too, am bringing you offer-

ings, while all the others are at prayers. Here they
are: ashes from the hearth, peelings, scraps of offal
crawling with maggots, a chunk of bread too filthy
even for our pigs. But your darling flies will love it,
won't they, Zeus? A good feast-day to you, old idol,
and let's hope it is your last. I'm not strong enough
to pull you down. All I can do is to spit at you. But
some day he will come, the man I'm waiting for, carrying a long, keen sword. He'll look you up and
down and chuckle, with his hands on his hips, like
this, and his head thrown back. Then he'll draw his
sword and chop you in two, from top to bottom—
like this! So the two halves of Zeus will fall apart,
one to the left, one to the right, and everyone will
see he's made of common wood. Just a lump of
cheap white deal, the terrible God of Death! And
all that frightfulness, the blood on his face, his dark-
green eyes, and all the rest—they'll see it was only a
coat of paint. *You*, anyhow, you know you're white
inside, white as a child's body, and you know, too,
that a sword can rip you limb from limb, and you
won't even bleed. Just a log of deal—anyhow it will
serve to light our fires next winter. [*She notices*
ORESTES.] Oh!

ORESTES : Don't be alarmed.

ELECTRA : I'm not alarmed. Not a bit. Who are you?

ORESTES : A stranger.

ELECTRA : Then you are welcome. All that's foreign to
this town is dear to me. Your name?

ORESTES : Philebus. I've come from Corinth.

ELECTRA : Ah? From Corinth. My name's Electra.

ORESTES : Electra— [*To the* TUTOR] Leave us.
[*Exit the* TUTOR.]

ELECTRA : Why are you looking at me like that ?

ORESTES : You're very beautiful. Not at all like the people in these parts.

ELECTRA : I beautiful ? Can you really mean it ? As beautiful as the Corinthian girls ?

ORESTES : Yes.

ELECTRA : Well, here they never tell me that I'm beautiful. Perhaps they don't want me to know it. Anyhow, what use would beauty be to me ? I'm only a servant.

ORESTES : What ! You a servant ?

ELECTRA : The least of the servants in the palace. I wash the King's and the Queen's underlinen. And how dirty it is, all covered with spots and stains ! Yes, I have to wash everything they wear next their skin, the shifts they wrap their rotting bodies in, the nightdresses Clytemnestra has on when the King shares her bed. I shut my eyes and scrub with all my might. I have to wash up, too. You don't believe me ? See my hands, all chapped and rough. Why are you looking at them in that funny way ? Do they, by any chance, look like the hands of a princess ?

ORESTES : Poor little hands. No, they don't look like a princess's hands. . . . But tell me more. What else do they make you do ?

ELECTRA : Every morning I've to empty the ash-can. I drag it out of the palace, and then—well, you saw what I do with the refuse. That big fellow in wood is Zeus, God of Death and Flies. The other day, when the High Priest came here to make his usual bows and scrapings, he found himself treading on cabbage-stumps and rotten turnips and mussel-shells. He looked startled, I can tell you! I say! You won't tell on me, will you?

ORESTES: No.

ELECTRA: Really I don't care if you do. They can't make things much worse for me than they are already. I'm used to being beaten. Perhaps they'd shut me up in one of the rooms in the tower. That wouldn't be so bad; at least I wouldn't have to see their faces. Just imagine what I get by way of thanks at bedtime, when my day's work is done. I go up to a tall, stout lady with dyed hair, with thick lips and very white hands, a queen's hands, that smell of honey. Then she puts her hands on my shoulders and dabs my forehead with her lips and says: "Good night, Electra. Good night." Every evening. Every evening I have to feel that woman slobbering on my face. Ugh! Like a piece of raw meat on my forehead. But I hold myself up, I've never fallen yet. She's my mother, you know. If I was up in the tower, she wouldn't kiss me any more.

ORESTES: Have you never thought of running away?

ELECTRA: I haven't the courage; I daren't face the country roads at night all by myself.

ORESTES: Is there no one, no girl friend of yours, who'd go with you?

ELECTRA: No, I am quite alone. Ask any of the people here, and they'll tell you I'm a pest, a public nuisance. I've no friends.

◇◇

ORESTES : Not even an old nurse, who saw you into the world and has kept a little affection for you ?

ELECTRA : Not even an old nurse. Mother will tell you; I freeze even the kindest hearts—that's how I am.

ORESTES : Do you propose to spend your life here ?

ELECTRA [*excitedly*] : My life ? Oh no, no ! Of course not ! Listen. I'm waiting for—for something.

ORESTES : Something, or someone ?

ELECTRA : That's my secret. Now it's your turn to speak. You're good-looking, too. Will you be here long ?

ORESTES : Well, I'd thought of leaving today. But, as it is—

ELECTRA : Yes ?

ORESTES : As it is, I'm not so sure.

ELECTRA : Is Corinth a pretty place ?

ORESTES : Very pretty.

ELECTRA : Do you like it ? Are you proud of Corinth ?

ORESTES : Yes.

ELECTRA : How strange that sounds ! I can't imagine myself being proud of my home town. Tell me what it feels like.

ORESTES : Well— No, I don't know. I can't explain.

ELECTRA : You can't ? I wonder why. [*A short silence.*] What's Corinth like ? Are there shady streets and squares ? Places where one can stroll in the cool of the evening ?

ORESTES : Yes.

ELECTRA : And everyone comes out of doors ? People go for walks together ?

ORESTES: Almost everyone is out and about at sundown.

ELECTRA: Boys and girls together?

ORESTES: Oh yes, one often sees them going for walks together.

ELECTRA: And they always find something to say to each other? They like each other's company, and one hears them laughing in the streets quite late at night?

ORESTES: Yes.

ELECTRA: I suppose you think I'm very childish. But it's so hard for me to picture a life like that—going for walks, laughing and singing in the streets. Everybody here is sick with fear. Everyone except me. And I—

ORESTES: Yes? And you?

ELECTRA: Oh, I—I'm sick with—hatred. And what do they do all day, the girls at Corinth?

ORESTES: Well, they spend quite a while making themselves pretty; then they sing or play on lutes. Then they call on their friends, and at night they go to dances.

ELECTRA: But don't they have any worries?

ORESTES: Only quite little ones.

ELECTRA: Yes? Now listen well, please. Don't the people at Corinth feel remorse?

ORESTES: Sometimes. Not very often.

ELECTRA: So they do what they like and, afterwards, don't give another thought to it?

ORESTES: That's their way.

◇◇◇

ELECTRA: How strange! [*A short silence.*] Please tell me something else; I want to know it because of— of someone I'm expecting. Suppose one of the young fellows you've been telling about, who walk and laugh with girls in the evenings—suppose one of these young men came home after a long journey and found his father murdered, and his mother living with the murderer, and his sister treated like a slave —what would he do, that young man from Corinth? Would he just take it for granted and slink out of his father's house and look for consolation with his girl friends? Or would he draw his sword and hurl himself at the assassin, and slash his brains out? . . . Why are you silent?

ORESTES: I was wondering—

ELECTRA: What? You can't say what he'd do?

CLYTEMNESTRA [*off stage, calling*]: Electra!

ELECTRA: Hush!

ORESTES: What is it?

ELECTRA: That was my mother, Queen Clytemnestra. [CLYTEMNESTRA *enters.*] What's this, Philebus? Are you afraid of her?

ORESTES [*to himself*]: So that's the face I tried to picture, night after night, until I came to see it, really *see* it, drawn and haggard under the rosy mask of paint. But I hadn't counted on those dead eyes.

CLYTEMNESTRA: Electra, hear the King's order. You are to make ready for the ceremony. You must wear your black dress and your jewels. . . . Well, what does this behavior mean? Why are you pressing

your elbows to your hips and staring at the ground?
Oh, I know your tricks, my girl, but they don't de-
ceive me any longer. Just now I was watching at the
window and I saw a very different Electra, a girl
with flashing eyes, bold gestures. . . . Why don't
you answer?

ELECTRA: Do you really think a scullery-maid would
add to the splendor of your festival?

CLYTEMNESTRA: No play-acting. You are a princess,
Electra, and the townsfolk expect to see you, as in
former years.

ELECTRA: A princess—yes, the princess of a day. Once
a year, when this day comes round, you remember
who I am; because, of course, the people want an
edifying glimpse of our family life. A strange princess, indeed, who herds pigs and washes up. Tell me,
will Ægistheus put his arm round my neck as he did
last time? Will he smile tenderly on me, while he
mumbles horrible threats in my ear?

CLYTEMNESTRA: If you would have him otherwise, it
rests with you.

ELECTRA: Yes—if I let myself be tainted by your remorse; if I beg the gods' forgiveness for a crime I
never committed. Yes—if I kiss your royal husband's hand and call him father. Ugh! The mere
thought makes me sick. There's dry blood under his
nails.

CLYTEMNESTRA: Do as you will. I have long ceased
giving you orders in my name. It is the King's command I bring you.

ELECTRA : And why should I obey him? Ægistheus is your husband, Mother, your dearly beloved husband —not mine.

CLYTEMNESTRA : That is all I have to say, Electra. Only too well I see you are determined to bring ruin on yourself, and on us all. Yet who am I to counsel you, I who ruined my whole life in a single morning? You hate me, my child, but what disturbs me more is your likeness to me, as I was once. I used to have those clean-cut features, that fever in the blood, those smoldering eyes—and nothing good came of them.

ELECTRA : No! Don't say I'm like you! Tell me, Philebus—you can see us side by side—am I really like her?

ORESTES : How can I tell? Her face is like a pleasant garden that hail and storms have ravaged. And upon yours I see a threat of storm; one day passion will sear it to the bone.

ELECTRA : A threat of storm? Good! So far I welcome the likeness. May your words come true!

CLYTEMNESTRA : And you, young man, who stare so boldly at us, who are you and why have you come here? Let me look at you more closely.

ELECTRA [*quickly*] : He's a Corinthian, of the name of Philebus. A traveler.

CLYTEMNESTRA : Philebus? Ah!

ELECTRA : You seemed to fear another name.

CLYTEMNESTRA : To fear? If the doom I brought on my life has taught me anything, it is that I have nothing left to fear. . . . Welcome to Argos, stranger.

Yes, come nearer. How young you seem! What's your age?

ORESTES: Eighteen.

CLYTEMNESTRA: Are your parents alive?

ORESTES: My father's dead.

CLYTEMNESTRA: And your mother? Is she about my age? Ah, you don't answer. I suppose she looks much younger; she still laughs and sings when you are with her. Do you love her? Answer me, please. Why did you leave her?

ORESTES: I am on my way to Sparta, to enlist in the army.

CLYTEMNESTRA: Most travelers give our city a wide berth. Some go twenty leagues out of their way to avoid it. Were you not warned? The people of the Plain have put us in quarantine; they see our repentance as a sort of pestilence and are afraid of being infected.

ORESTES: I know.

CLYTEMNESTRA: Did they tell you that we bear the burden of an inexpiable crime, committed fifteen years ago?

ORESTES: Yes, they told me that.

CLYTEMNESTRA: And that Queen Clytemnestra bears the heaviest load of guilt—that men shudder at her name?

ORESTES: That, too, I heard.

CLYTEMNESTRA: And yet you've come here! Stranger, I am Queen Clytemnestra.

ELECTRA: Don't pity her, Philebus. The Queen is indulging in our national pastime, the game of public

◇◇◇

confession. Here everyone cries his sins on the housetops. On holidays you'll often see a worthy shopkeeper dragging himself along on his knees, covering his hair with dust, and screaming out that he's a murderer, a libertine, a liar, and all the rest of it. But the folk of Argos are getting a little tired of these amusements; everyone knows his neighbor's sins by heart. The Queen's, especially, have lost interest; they're official—our basic crimes, in fact. So you can imagine her delight when she finds someone like you, somebody raw and young, who doesn't even know her name, to hear her tale of guilt. A marvelous opportunity ! It's as if she were confessing for the first time.

CLYTEMNESTRA : Be silent. Anyone has the right to spit in my face, to call me murderess and whore. But no one has the right to speak ill of my remorse.

ELECTRA : Note her words, Philebus. That's a rule of the game. People will beg you to condemn them, but you must be sure to judge them only on the sins they own to; their other evil deeds are no one's business, and they wouldn't thank you for detecting them.

CLYTEMNESTRA : Fifteen years ago men said I was the loveliest woman in Greece. Look at me now and judge my sufferings. Let me be frank, young stranger; it is not the death of that old lecher that I regret. When I saw his blood tingeing the water in the bath, I sang and danced for joy. And even now, after fifteen years, whenever I recall it, I have a thrill of pleasure. But—but I had a son; he would be your age now. When Ægistheus handed him over to his bravoes, I—

ELECTRA: You had a daughter too, my mother, if I'm not mistaken. And you've made of her a scullion. But that crime, it seems, sits lightly on your conscience.

CLYTEMNESTRA: You are young, Electra. It is easy for young people, who have not yet had a chance of sinning, to condemn. But wait, my girl; one day you, too, will be trailing after you an inexpiable crime. At every step you will think that you are leaving it behind, but it will remain as heavy as before. Whenever you look back you will see it there, just at arm's length, glowing darkly like a black crystal. And you will have forgotten what it really is, and murmur to yourself: "It wasn't I, it could not have been I, who did that." Yet, though you disown it time and time again, always it will be there, a dead weight holding you back. And then at last you will realize that you staked your life on a single throw of the dice, and nothing remains for you but to drag your crime after you until you die. For that is the law, just or unjust, of repentance. Ah, then we'll see a change come over your young pride.

ELECTRA: My *young* pride? So it's your lost youth you are regretting, still more than your crime. It's my youth you detest, even more than my innocence.

CLYTEMNESTRA: What I detest in you, Electra, is— myself. Not your youth—far from it!—but my own.

◇◇

ELECTRA: And I—it's you, it's *you* I hate.

CLYTEMNESTRA: For shame, Electra! Here we are, scolding each other like two women of the same age in love with the same man! And yet I am your mother. . . . I do not know who you are, young man, nor what brings you here, but your presence bodes no good. Electra hates me—that, of course, I always knew. But for fifteen years we have kept the peace; only our eyes betrayed our feelings. And now you have come, you have spoken, and here we are showing our teeth and snapping at each other like two curs in the street. An ancient law of Argos compels us to give you hospitality, but, I make no secret of it, I had rather you were gone. As for you, my child, too faithful copy of myself, 'tis true I have no love for you. But I had rather cut off my right hand than do you harm. Only too well you know it, and you trade on my weakness. But I advise you not to rear your noxious little head against Ægistheus; he has a short way with vipers. Mark my words, do his bidding—or you will rue it.

ELECTRA: Tell the King that I shall not attend the rite. Do you know what they do, Philebus? Above the town there's a great cavern; none of our young men, not even the bravest, has ever found its end. People say that it leads down to hell, and the High Priest has had the entrance blocked with a great stone. Well—would you believe it?—each year when this anniversary comes round, the townspeople gather outside the cavern, soldiers roll away the stone, and our dead, so they say, come up from hell and roam the city. Places are laid for them at every table, chairs and beds made ready, and the people in the house huddle in corners to make room for them during the night-watches. For the dead are everywhere, the whole town's at their mercy. You can imagine how our townsfolk plead with them. "My poor dead darling, I didn't mean to wrong you. Please be kind." Tomorrow, at cock-crow, they'll return underground, the stone will be rolled back, and that will be the end of it until this day next year. Well, I refuse to take part in this mummery. Those dead folk are *their* dead, not mine.

CLYTEMNESTRA: If you will not obey his summons willingly, the King will have you brought to him by force.

ELECTRA: By force? . . . . I see. Very well, then. My good, kind mother, will you please tell the King that I shall certainly obey. I shall attend the rite, and if the townsfolk wish to see me, they won't be disappointed. . . . Philebus, will you do something for me? Please don't go at once, but stay here for the ceremony. Perhaps some parts of it may entertain you. Now I'll go and make myself ready.

[*Exit* ELECTRA.]

CLYTEMNESTRA [*to* ORESTES]: Leave this place. I feel that you are going to bring disaster on us. You have no cause to wish us ill; we have done nothing to you. So go, I beg you. By all you hold most sacred, for your mother's sake, I beg you, go.

[*Exit* CLYTEMNESTRA.]

ORESTES [*thoughtfully*]: For my mother's sake.

◇◇◇

[ZEUS *enters and comes up to him.*]

ZEUS: Your attendant tells me you wish to leave. He has been looking for horses all over Argos, but can find none. Well, I can procure for you two sturdy mares and riding-gear at a very low figure.

ORESTES: I've changed my mind. I am not leaving Argos.

ZEUS [*meditatively*]: Ah, so you're not leaving, after all. [*A short pause. Then, in a quicker tempo*] In that case I shall stay with you and be your host. I know an excellent inn in the lower town where we can lodge together. You won't regret my company, I can assure you. But first—Abraxas, galla, galla, tsay, tsay—let me rid you of those flies. A man of my age can often be very helpful to lads like you. I'm old enough to be your father; you must tell me all about yourself and your troubles. So come, young man, don't try to shake me off. Meetings like this are often of more use than one would think. Consider the case of Telemachus—you know whom I mean, King Ulysses' son. One fine day he met an old worthy of the name of Mentor, who joined forces with him. Now I wonder if you know who that old fellow Mentor really was. . . .

[*He escorts* ORESTES *off the stage, holding him in conversation, while the curtain falls.*]

A C T   I I

SCENE I

*A mountain terrace, with a cavern on the right. Its en-
trance is blocked by a large black boulder. On the
left is a flight of steps leading up to a temple. A
crowd of men and women have gathered for the
ceremony.*

A WOMAN [*kneeling before her little son, as she
straightens the kerchief round his neck*]: There!
That's the third time I've had to straighten it for you.
[*She dusts his clothes.*] That's better. Now try to behave properly, and mind you start crying when
you're told.

THE CHILD: Is that where they come from?

THE WOMAN: Yes.

THE CHILD: I'm frightened.

THE WOMAN: And so you should be, darling. Terribly
frightened. That's how one grows up into a decent,
god-fearing man.

A MAN: They'll have good weather today.

ANOTHER MAN: Just as well. It seems they still like sunlight, shadows though they are. Last year, when it
rained, they were fierce, weren't they?

FIRST MAN: Ay, that's the word. Fierce.

SECOND MAN: A shocking time we had!

THIRD MAN: Once they've gone back to their cave and

left us to ourselves, I'll climb up here again and look at that there stone, and I'll say to myself: "Now we've a year's peace before us."

FOURTH MAN : Well, I'm not like you, I ain't consoled that easily. From tomorrow I'll start wondering how they'll be next year. Every year they're getting nastier and nastier, and—

SECOND MAN : Hold your tongue, you fool! Suppose one of them has crept out through a crevice and is prowling round us now, eavesdropping, like. There's some of the Dead come out ahead of time, so I've heard tell.

[*They eye each other nervously.*]

A YOUNG WOMAN : If only it would start! What are they up to, those palace folk? They're never in a hurry, and it's all this waiting gets one down, what with the blazing sun and only that big black stone to look at. Just think! They're all there, crowded up behind the stone, gloating over the cruel things they're going to do to us.

AN OLD WOMAN : That's enough, my girl. . . . We all know she's no better than she should be; that's why she's so scared of her ghost. Her husband died last spring, and for ten years she'd been fooling the poor man.

YOUNG WOMAN : I don't deny it. Sure enough, I fooled him to the top of his bent; but I always liked him and I led him a pleasant life, that he can't deny. He never knew a thing about the other men, and when he died, you should have seen the way he looked at me, so tenderly, like a grateful dog. Of course, he knows

◇◇

everything now, and it's bitter pain for him, poor fellow, and all his love has turned to hate. Presently I'll feel him coiling round me, like a wisp of smoke, and he'll cling to me more closely than any living man has ever clung. I'll bring him home with me, wound round my neck like a tippet. I've a tasty little meal all ready, with the cakes and honey that he always liked. But it's all no use, I know. He'll never forgive me, and tonight—oh, how I dread it! —he will share my bed.

A MAN: Ay, she's right. What's Ægistheus doing? We can't bear this suspense much longer. It ain't fair to keep us waiting like this.

ANOTHER MAN: Sorry for yourself, are you? But do you think Ægistheus is less afraid than we? Tell me, how'd you like to be in his shoes, and have Agamemnon gibbering at you for twenty-four hours?

YOUNG WOMAN: Oh, this horrible, horrible suspense! Do you know, I have a feeling that all of you are drifting miles and miles away, leaving me alone. The stone is not yet rolled aside, but each of us is shut up with his dead, and lonely as a raindrop.

[ZEUS *enters, followed by* ORESTES *and* THE TUTOR.]

ZEUS: This way, young man; you'll have a better view.

ORESTES: So here we have them, the citizens of Argos, King Agamemnon's loyal subjects!

THE TUTOR: What an ugly lot! Observe, young master, their sallow cheeks and sunken eyes. These folk are perishing of fear. What better example could we have of the effects of superstition? Just look at them! And if you need another proof of the soundness of my teaching, look on me and my rosy cheeks.

ZEUS: Much good they do you, your pink cheeks. For all your roses, my good man, you're no more than a sack of dung, like all those others, in the eyes of Zeus. Yes, though you may not guess it, you stink to heaven. These folk, at least, are wise in their generation; they know how bad they smell.

A MAN [*climbing on to the temple steps, harangues the crowd*]: Do they want to drive us mad? Let's raise our voices all together and summon Ægistheus. Make him understand we will not suffer any more delay.

THE CROWD: Ægistheus! King Ægistheus! Have pity on us!

A WOMAN: Pity, yes, pity, you cry. And will none have pity on me? He'll come with his slit throat, the man I loathed so bitterly, and clammy, unseen arms will maul me in the darkness, all through the night.

ORESTES: But this is madness! Why doesn't someone tell these wretched people—?

ZEUS: What's this, young man? Why this ado over a woman who's lost her nerve? Wait and see; there's worse to come.

A MAN [*falling on his knees*]: I stink! Oh, how I stink! I am a mass of rottenness. See how the flies are teeming round me, like carrion crows. . . . That's right, my harpies; sting and gouge and scavenge me; bore through my flesh to my black heart. I have sinned a thousand times, I am a sink of ordure, and I reek to heaven.

◇◇◇

ZEUS: O worthy man!

SOME MEN [*helping him to his feet*] : That's enough. You shall talk about it later, when *they* are out.

[*Gasping, rolling his eyes, the man stares at them.*]

THE CROWD: Ægistheus! Ægistheus! For mercy's sake, give the order to begin. We can bear no more.

[ÆGISTHEUS *comes on to the temple steps, followed by* CLYTEMNESTRA, THE HIGH PRIEST, *and* BODY-GUARDS.]

ÆGISTHEUS: Dogs! How dare you bewail your lot? Have you forgotten your disgrace? Then, by Zeus, I shall refresh your memories. [*He turns to* CLYTEM-NESTRA.] We must start without her, it seems. But let her beware! My punishment will be condign.

CLYTEMNESTRA: She promised to attend. No doubt she is making ready, lingering in front of her mirror.

ÆGISTHEUS [*to the soldiers*] : Go seek Electra in the palace and bring her here by force, if need be. [SOLDIERS *file out. He addresses* THE CROWD.] Take your usual places. The men on my right, women and children on my left. Good.

[*A short silence.* ÆGISTHEUS *is waiting.*]

HIGH PRIEST: Sire, these people are at breaking-point.

ÆGISTHEUS: I know. But I am waiting for—

[*The* SOLDIERS *return.*]

A SOLDIER: Your Majesty, we have searched for the princess everywhere. But there is no one in the palace.

ÆGISTHEUS: So be it. We shall deal with her tomorrow. [*To the* HIGH PRIEST] Begin.

HIGH PRIEST: Roll away the stone.

✧✧

THE CROWD : Ah !

[*The* SOLDIERS *roll away the stone. The* HIGH PRIEST *goes to the entrance of the cavern.*]

HIGH PRIEST : You, the forgotten and forsaken, all you whose hopes were dupes, who creep along the ground darkling like smoke wraiths and have nothing left you but your great shame—you, the dead, arise; this is your day of days. Come up, pour forth like a thick cloud of fumes of brimstone driven by the wind; rise from the bowels of the earth, ye who have died a hundred deaths, ye whom every heartbeat in our breasts strikes dead again. In the name of anger unappeased and unappeasable, and the lust of vengeance, I summon you to wreak your hatred on the living. Come forth and scatter like a dark miasma in our streets, weave between the mother and her child, the lover and his beloved; make us regret that we, too, are not dead. Arise, spectres, harpies, ghouls, and goblins of our nights. Soldiers, arise, who died blaspheming; arise, downtrodden victims, children of disgrace; arise, all ye who died of hunger, whose last sigh was a curse. See, the living are here to greet you, fodder for your wrath. Arise and have at them like a great rushing wind, and gnaw them to the bone. Arise ! Arise ! Arise !

[*A tomtom sounds, and the* PRIEST *dances at the entrance of the cavern, slowly at first, then quickening his gyrations until he falls to the ground exhausted.*]

ÆGISTHEUS : They are coming forth.

THE CROWD : Heaven help us !

◇◇

ORESTES : I can bear this no longer. I must go—

ZEUS : Look at me, young man. In the eyes. Good; you understand. Now, keep quiet.

ORESTES : Who—who are you?

ZEUS : You shall know soon.

[ÆGISTHEUS *comes slowly down the temple steps.*]

ÆGISTHEUS : They are there. All of them. [*A short silence.*] There he is, Aricië, the husband you used so ill. There he is, beside you, kissing you tenderly, clasping you in his dead arms. How he loves you! And, ah, how he hates you! . . . There she is, Nicias, your mother, who died of your neglect. . . . And you there, Segestes, you bloodsucker—they are all round you, the wretched men who borrowed of you; those who starved to death, and those who hanged themselves because of you. In your debt they died, but today they are your creditors. And you, fathers and mothers, loving parents, lower your eyes humbly. They are there, your dead children, stretching their frail arms towards you, and all the happiness you denied them, all the tortures you inflicted, weigh like lead on their sad, childish, unforgiving hearts.

THE CROWD : Have mercy!

ÆGISTHEUS : Mercy? You ask for mercy? Do you not know the dead have no mercy? Their grievances are timeproof, adamant; rancor without end. Do you hope, Nicias, to atone by deeds of kindness for the wrong you did your mother? But what act of kindness can ever reach her now? Her soul is like a sultry, windless noon, in which nothing stirs, noth-

◇◇◇

ing changes, nothing lives. Only a fierce unmoving sun beats down on bare rocks forever. The dead have ceased to be—think what that implies in all its ruthlessness—yes, they are no more, and in their eternal keeping your crimes have no reprieve.

THE CROWD: Mercy!

ÆGISTHEUS: Well you may cry mercy! Play your parts, you wretched mummers, for today you have a full house to watch you. Millions of staring, hopeless eyes are brooding darkly on your faces and your gestures. They can see us, read our hearts, and we are naked in the presence of the dead. Ah, that makes you squirm; it burns and sears you, that stern, calm gaze unchanging as the gaze of eyes remembered.

THE CROWD: Mercy!

THE MEN: Forgive us for living while you are dead.

THE WOMEN: Have mercy! Tokens of you are ever with us, we see your faces everywhere we turn. We wear mourning unceasingly, and weep for you from dawn till dusk, from dusk till dawn. But somehow, try as we may, your memory dwindles and slips through our fingers; daily it grows dimmer and we know ourselves the guiltier. Yes, you are leaving us, ebbing away like life-blood from a wound. And yet, know you well—if this can mollify your bitter hatred—that you, our dear departed, have laid waste our lives.

THE MEN: Forgive us for living while you are dead.

THE CHILDREN: Please forgive us. We didn't want to be born, we're ashamed of growing up. What wrong can we have done you? It's not our fault if we're alive. And only just alive; see how small we are, how pale and puny. We never laugh or sing, we glide about like ghosts. And we're so frightened of you, so terribly afraid. Have mercy on us.

THE MEN : Forgive us for living while you are dead.

ÆGISTHEUS : Hold your peace! If you voice your sorrow thus, what will be left for me, your King, to say? For my ordeal has begun; the earth is quaking, and the light failing, and the greatest of the dead is coming forth—he whom I slew with my own hand, King Agamemnon.

ORESTES [*drawing his sword*] : I forbid you to drag my father's name into this mummery.

ZEUS [*clutching his arms*] : Stop, young fellow! Stop that!

ÆGISTHEUS [*Looking round*] : Who dares to—? [ELECTRA, *wearing a white dress, comes on to the temple steps.* ÆGISTHEUS *sees her.*] Electra!

THE CROWD : Electra!

ÆGISTHEUS : What is the meaning of this, Electra? Why are you in white?

ELECTRA : It's my prettiest dress. The city holds high festival today, and I thought I'd look my best.

HIGH PRIEST : Would you insult our dead? This day is *their* day, and well you know it. You should be in mourning.

ELECTRA : Why? I'm not afraid of *my* dead, and yours mean nothing to me.

ÆGISTHEUS : That is so; your dead are not our dead. . . . Remember the breed she comes of, the breed of Atreus, who treacherously cut his nephews' throats. What are you, Electra, but the last survivor of an accursed race? Ay, that whorish dress becomes you. I suffered your presence in the palace out of pity, but now I know I erred; the old foul blood of the house of Atreus flows in your veins. And if I did not see to it, you would taint us all. But bide awhile, my girl, and you will learn how I can punish. Your eyes will be red with weeping for many a day.

THE CROWD: Sacrilege! Sacrilege! Away with her!

ÆGISTHEUS: Hear, miserable girl, the murmurs of these good folk you have outraged. Were I not here to curb their anger, they would tear you in pieces.

THE CROWD: Away with her, the impious wretch!

ELECTRA: Is it impious to be gay? Why can't these good folk of yours be gay? What prevents them?

ÆGISTHEUS: She is laughing, the wanton—and her dead father is standing there, with blood on his face.

ELECTRA: How dare you talk of Agamemnon? How can you be so sure he doesn't visit me by night and tell me all his secrets? Ah, if you knew the love and longing that hoarse, dead voice breathes in my ears! Yes, I'm laughing—laughing for the first time in my life; for the first time I'm happy. And can you be so sure my new-won happiness doesn't rejoice my father's heart? More likely, if he's here and sees his daughter in her white dress—his daughter of whom you've made a wretched drudge—if he sees her holding her head high, keeping her pride intact, more likely the last thing he dreams of is to blame me. No, his eyes are sparkling in the havoc of his face, he's twisting his blood-stained lips in the shadow of a smile.

THE YOUNG WOMAN: Can it be true, what she says?

VOICES: No, no. She's talking nonsense. She's gone mad. Electra, go, for pity's sake, or your sins will be visited on us.

ELECTRA: But what is it you're so frightened of? I can see all round you and there's nothing but your own shadows. Now listen to what I've just been told, something you may not know. In Greece there are cities where men live happily. White, contented cities, basking like lizards in the sun. At this very moment, under this same sky, children are playing in the streets of Corinth. And their mothers aren't asking forgiveness for having brought them into the world. No, they're smiling tenderly at them, they're proud of their motherhood. Mothers of Argos, can't you understand? Does it mean nothing to you, the pride of a mother who looks at her son and thinks: "It's I who bore him, brought him up"?

ÆGISTHEUS: That's enough. Keep silent, or I'll thrust your words down your throat.

VOICES: Yes, yes. Make her stop. She's talked enough.

OTHER VOICES: No, let her speak. It's Agamemnon speaking through her.

ELECTRA: The sun is shining. Everywhere down in the plains men are looking up and saying: "It's a fine day," and they're happy. Are you so set on making yourselves wretched that you've forgotten the simple joy of the peasant who says as he walks across his fields: "It's a fine day"? No, there you stand, hanging your heads, moping and mumbling, more dead than alive. You're too terrified to lift a finger, afraid of jolting your precious ghosts if you make any movement. That would be dreadful, wouldn't it, if your hand suddenly went through a patch of clammy mist, and it was your grandmother's ghost! Now look at me. I'm spreading out my arms freely, and I'm stretching like someone just roused from sleep. I have my place in the sunlight, my full place and to spare. And does the sky fall on my head? Now I'm dancing, see, I'm dancing, and all I feel is the wind's breath fanning my cheeks. Where are the dead? Do you think they're dancing with me, in step?

HIGH PRIEST: People of Argos, I tell you that this woman is a profaner of all we hold most holy. Woe to her and to all of you who listen to her words!

ELECTRA: Oh, my beloved dead—Iphigeneia, my elder sister, and Agamemnon, my father and my only King —hear my prayer. If I am an evil-doer, if I offend your sorrowing shades, make some sign that I may know. But if, my dear ones, you approve, let no leaf stir, no blade of grass be moved, and no sound break in on my sacred dance. For I am dancing for joy, for peace among men; I dance for happiness and life. My dead ones, I invoke your silence that these people around me may know your hearts are with me.

[*She dances.*]

VOICES IN THE CROWD: Look how she's dancing, light as a flame. Look how her dress is rippling, like a

◇◇◇

banner in the wind. And the Dead—the Dead do nothing.

THE YOUNG WOMAN : And see her look of ecstasy—oh, no, no, that's not the face of a wicked woman. Well, Ægistheus, what have you to say ? Why are you silent ?

ÆGISTHEUS : I waste no words on her. Does one argue with malignant vermin ? No, one stamps them out. My kindness to her in the past was a mistake, but a mistake that can be remedied. Have no fear, I shall make short work of her and end her accursed race.

VOICES IN THE CROWD : Answer us, King Ægistheus. Threats are no answer.

THE YOUNG WOMAN : She's dancing, smiling, oh, so happily, and the dead seem to protect her. Oh fortunate, too fortunate Electra ! Look, I, too, am holding out my arms, baring my neck to the sunlight.

A VOICE IIN THE CROWD : The Dead hold their peace. Ægistheus, you have lied.

ORESTES : Dear Electra !

ZEUS : This is too much. I'll shut that foolish wench's tongue. [*Stretches out his right arm.*] Poseidon, carabou, carabou, roola. [*The big stone which blocked the entrance to the cavern rumbles across the stage and crashes against the temple steps.* ELECTRA *stops dancing.*]

THE CROWD : Ah ! . . . Mercy on us !

[*A long silence.*]

HIGH PRIEST : Froward and fickle race, now you have seen how the Dead avenge themselves. Mark how the flies are beating down on you, in thick, swirling

❖❖❖

clouds. You have hearkened to the tempter's voice, and a curse has fallen on the city.

THE CROWD: It is not our fault, we are innocent. That woman came and tempted us, with her lying tongue. To the river with her! Drown the witch.

AN OLD WOMAN [*pointing to the* YOUNG WOMAN]: That young huzzy there was lapping up her words like milk. Strip her naked and lash her till she squeals. [*The* WOMEN *seize the* YOUNG WOMAN, *while the* MEN *surge up the temple steps, towards* ELECTRA.]

ÆGISTHEUS [*straightening up*]: Silence, dogs! Back to your places! Vengeance is mine, not yours. [*A short silence.*] Well, you have seen what comes of disobeying me. Henceforth you will know better than to misdoubt your ruler. Disperse to your homes, the Dead will keep you company and be your guests until tomorrow's dawn. Make place for them at your tables, at your hearths, and in your beds. And see that your good behavior blots out the memory of what has happened here. As for me—grieved though I am by your mistrust, I forgive you. But you, Electra—

ELECTRA: Yes? What of it? I failed to bring it off this time. Next time I'll do better.

ÆGISTHEUS: There shall be no next time. The custom of the city forbids my punishing you on the day the Dead are with us. This you knew, and you took advantage of it. But you are no longer one of us; I cast you out forever. You shall go hence barefooted, with nothing in your hands, wearing that shameless dress. And I hereby order any man who sees you within our gates after the sun has risen to strike you down and rid the city of its bane.

[*He goes out, followed by* THE SOLDIERS. THE CROWD *file past* ELECTRA, *shaking their fists at her.*]

ZEUS [*to* ORESTES] : Well, young master, were you duly edified? For, unless I'm much mistaken, the tale has a moral. The wicked have been punished and the good rewarded. [*He points to* ELECTRA.] As for that woman—

ORESTES [*sharply*] : Mind what you say. That woman is my sister. Now go; I want to talk to her.

ZEUS [*observes him for a moment, then shrugs his shoulders*] : Very good.

[*Exit* ZEUS, *followed by* THE TUTOR.]

ORESTES : Electra!

ELECTRA [*Still standing on the temple steps, she raises her eyes and gazes at him.*] : Ah, you're still there, Philebus?

ORESTES : You're in danger, Electra. You mustn't stay a moment longer in this city.

ELECTRA : In danger? Yes, that's true. You saw how I failed to bring it off. It was a bit your fault, you know—but I'm not angry with you.

ORESTES : My fault? How?

ELECTRA : You deceived me. [*She comes down the steps towards him.*] Let me look at your eyes. Yes, it was your eyes that made a fool of me.

ORESTES : There's no time to lose. Listen, Electra! We'll escape together. Someone's getting a horse for me and you can ride pillion.

ELECTRA : No.

ORESTES : What ? You won't come away with me ?

ELECTRA : I refuse to run away.

ORESTES : I'll take you with me to Corinth.

ELECTRA [*laughing*] : Corinth ? Exactly ! I know you mean well, but you're fooling me again. What could a girl like me do in Corinth ? I've got to keep a level head, you know. Only yesterday my desires were so simple, so modest. When I waited at table, with meek, downcast eyes, I used to watch the two of them—the handsome old woman with the dead face, and the fat, pale King with the slack mouth and that absurd beard like a regiment of spiders running round his chin. And then I'd dream of what I'd see one day—a wisp of steam, like one's breath on a cold morning, rising from their split bellies. That was the only thing I lived for, Philebus, I assure you. I don't know what you're after, but this I know : that I mustn't believe you. Your eyes are too bold for my liking. . . . Do you know what I used to tell myself before I met you ? That a wise person can want nothing better from life than to pay back the wrong that has been done him.

ORESTES : If you come with me, Electra, you'll see there are many, many other things to ask of life—without one's ceasing to be wise.

ELECTRA : No, I won't listen any more ; you've done me quite enough harm already. You came here with your kind, girlish face and your eager eyes—and you made me forget my hatred. I unlocked my hands and I let my one and only treasure slip through them. You lured me into thinking one could cure the

people here by words. Well, you saw what happened. They nurse their disease; they've got to like
their sores so much that they scratch them with their
dirty nails to keep them festering. Words are no use
for such as they. An evil thing is conquered only by
another evil thing, and only violence can save them.
So good-by, Philebus, and leave me to my bad
dreams.

ORESTES: They'll kill you.

ELECTRA: We have a sanctuary here, Apollo's shrine.
Often criminals take shelter there, and so long as
they are in the temple, no one can touch a hair of
their heads. That's where I'll go.

ORESTES: But why refuse my help?

ELECTRA: It's not for you to help me. Someone else
will come, to set me free. [*A short silence.*] My
brother isn't dead; I know that. And I'm waiting
for his coming.

ORESTES: Suppose he doesn't come?

ELECTRA: He *will* come; he's bound to come. He is of
our stock, you see; he has crime and tragedy in his
blood, as I have—the bad blood of the house of
Atreus. I picture him as a big, strong man, a born
fighter, with bloodshot eyes like our father's, always
smoldering with rage. He, too, is doomed; tangled
up in his destiny, like a horse whose belly is ripped
open and his legs are caught up in his guts. And now
at every step he tears his bowels out. Yes, one day he
will come, this city draws him. Nothing can hinder
his coming, for it is here he can do the greatest harm,
and suffer the greatest harm. I often seem to see him

coming, with lowered head, sullen with pain, muttering angry words. He scares me; every night I see him in my dreams, and I wake screaming with terror. But I'm waiting for him and I love him. I must stay here to direct his rage—for I, anyhow, keep a clear head—to point to the guilty and say: "Those are they, Orestes. Strike!"

ORESTES: And suppose he isn't like that at all?

ELECTRA: How can he be otherwise? Don't forget he's the son of Agamemnon and Clytemnestra.

ORESTES: But mightn't he be weary of all that tale of wickedness and bloodshed; if, for instance, he'd been brought up in a happy, peaceful city?

ELECTRA: Then I'd spit in his face, and I'd say: "Go away, you cur; go and keep company where you belong, with women. But you're reckoning without your doom, poor fool. You're a grandson of Atreus, and you can't escape the heritage of blood. You prefer shame to crime; so be it. But Fate will come and hunt you down in your bed; you'll have the shame to start with, and then you will commit the crime, however much you shirk it."

ORESTES: Electra, I am Orestes.

ELECTRA [*with a cry*]: Oh! . . . You liar!

ORESTES: By the shades of my father, Agamemnon, I swear I am Orestes. [*A short silence.*] Well? Why don't you carry out your threat and spit in my face?

ELECTRA: How could I? [*She gazes at him earnestly.*] So those shining eyes, that noble forehead, are—my brother's! Orestes. . . . Oh, I'd rather you had stayed Philebus, and my brother was dead. [*Shyly*]

◇◇

Was it true, what you said about your having lived at Corinth?

ORESTES: No. I was brought up by some well-to-do Athenians.

ELECTRA: How young you look! Have you ever been in battle? Has that sword you carry ever tasted blood?

ORESTES: Never.

ELECTRA: It's strange. I felt less lonely when I didn't know you. I was waiting for the Orestes of my dream; always thinking of his strength and of my weakness. And now you're there before me; Orestes, the real Orestes, was you all the time. I look at you and I see we're just a boy and a girl, two young orphans. But, you know, I love you. More than I'd have loved the other Orestes.

ORESTES: Then, if you love me, come away. We'll leave this place together.

ELECTRA: Leave Argos? No. It's here the doom of the Atrides must be played out, and I am of the house of Atreus. I ask nothing of you. I've nothing more to ask of Philebus. But here I stay.

[ZEUS *enters, back stage, and takes cover to listen to them.*]

ORESTES: Electra, I'm Orestes, your brother. I, too, am of the house of Atreus, and my place is at your side.

ELECTRA: No. You're not my brother; you're a stranger. Orestes is dead, and so much the better for him. From now on I'll do homage to his shade, along with my father's and my sister's. You, Philebus, claim to be of our house. So be it! But can you truly say that

◇◇◇

you are one of *us*? Was *your* childhood darkened
by the shadow of a murder? No, more likely you
were a quiet little boy with happy, trustful eyes, the
pride of your adoptive father. Naturally you could
trust people—they always had a smile for you—just
as you could trust the solid friendly things around
you: tables, beds, and stairs. And because you were
rich, and always nicely dressed, and had lots of toys,
you must have often thought the world was quite a
nice world to live in, like a big warm bath in which
one can splash and loll contentedly. My childhood
was quite different. When I was six I was a drudge,
and I mistrusted everything and everyone. [*A short
pause.*] So go away, my noble-souled brother. I have
no use for noble souls; what I need is an accomplice.

ORESTES: How could I leave you all alone; above all,
now that you've lost even your last hope? . . .
What do you propose to do here?

ELECTRA: That's my business. Good-by, Philebus.

ORESTES: So you're driving me away? [*He takes some
steps, then halts and faces her.*] Is it my fault if I'm
not the fierce young swashbuckler you expected?
Him you'd have taken by the hand at once and said:
"Strike!" Of me you asked nothing. But, good
heavens, why should I be outcast by my own sister
—when I've not even been put to the test?

ELECTRA: No, Philebus, I could never lay such a load
upon a heart like yours; a heart that has no hatred
in it.

ORESTES: You are right. No hatred; but no love, either.
You, Electra, I might have loved. And yet—I won-

der. Love or hatred calls for self-surrender. He cuts
a fine figure, the warm-blooded, prosperous man,
solidly entrenched in his well-being, who one fine
day surrenders all to love—or to hatred; himself, his
house, his land, his memories. But who am I, and
what have I to surrender? I'm a mere shadow of a
man; of all the ghosts haunting this town today, none
is ghostlier than I. The only loves I've known were
phantom loves, rare and vacillating as will-o'-the-
wisps. The solid passions of the living were never
mine. Never! [*A short silence.*] But, oh, the shame
of it! Here I am, back in the town where I was born,
and my own sister disavows me. And now—where
shall I go? What city must I haunt?

ELECTRA: Isn't there some pretty girl waiting for you
—somewhere in the world?

ORESTES: Nobody is waiting for me anywhere. I
wander from city to city, a stranger to all others and
to myself, and the cities close again behind me like
the waters of a pool. If I leave Argos, what trace of
my coming will remain, except the cruel disappoint-
ment of your hope?

ELECTRA: You told me about happy towns—

ORESTES: What do I care for happiness? I want my
share of memories, my native soil, my place among
the men of Argos. [*A short silence.*] Electra, I shall
not leave Argos.

ELECTRA: Please, please, Philebus, go away. If you have
any love for me, go. It hurts me to think what may
come to you here—nothing but evil, that I know—
and your innocence would ruin all my plans.

◇◇

ORESTES: I shall not go.

ELECTRA: How can you think I'd let you stay beside me—you with your stubborn uprightness—to pass silent judgment on my acts? Oh, why are you so obstinate? Nobody wants you here.

ORESTES: It's my one chance, and you, Electra—surely you won't refuse it to me? Try to understand. I want to be a man who belongs to some place, a man among comrades. Only consider. Even the slave bent beneath his load, dropping with fatigue and staring dully at the ground a foot in front of him—why, even that poor slave can say he's in *his* town, as a tree is in a forest, or a leaf upon the tree. Argos is all around him, warm, compact, and comforting. Yes, Electra, I'd gladly be that slave and enjoy that feeling of drawing the city round me like a blanket and curling myself up in it. No, I shall not go.

ELECTRA: Even if you stayed a hundred years among us, you'd still be a stranger here, and lonelier than if you were tramping the highroads of Greece. The townspeople would be watching you all the time from the corner of an eye, and they'd lower their voices when you came near.

ORESTES: Is it really so hard to win a place among you? My sword can serve the city, and I have gold to help the needy.

ELECTRA: We are not short of captains, or of charitable souls.

ORESTES: In that case— [*He takes some steps away from her, with lowered eyes.* ZEUS *comes forward and gazes at him, rubbing his hands.* ORESTES *raises*

◇◇◇

his eyes heavenwards.] Ah, if only I knew which path to take! O Zeus, our Lord and King of Heaven, not often have I called on you for help, and you have shown me little favor; yet this you know: that I have always tried to act aright. But now I am weary and my mind is dark; I can no longer distinguish right from wrong. I need a guide to point my way. Tell me, Zeus, is it truly your will that a king's son, hounded from his city, should meekly school himself to banishment and slink away from his ancestral home like a whipped cur? I cannot think it. And yet—and yet you have forbidden the shedding of blood. . . . What have I said? Who spoke of blood-shed? . . . O Zeus, I beseech you, if meek acceptance, the bowed head and lowly heart are what you would have of me, make plain your will by some sign; for no longer can I see my path.

ZEUS [*aside*]: Ah, that's where I can help you, my young friend. Abraxas, abraxas, tsou, tsou.

[*Light flashes out round the stone.*]

ELECTRA [*laughing*]: Splendid! It's raining miracles today! See what comes of being a pious young man and asking counsel of the gods. [*She is convulsed with laughter and can hardly get the words out.*] Oh, noble youth, Philebus, darling of the gods! "Show me a sign," you asked. "Show me a sign." Well, now you've had your sign—a blaze of light round that precious, sacred stone of theirs. So off you go to Corinth! Off you go!

ORESTES [*staring at the stone*]: So that is the Right Thing. To live at peace—always at perfect peace. I

◊◊◊

see. Always to say "Excuse me," and "Thank you." That's what's wanted, eh? [*He stares at the stone in silence for some moments.*] The Right Thing. *Their* Right Thing. [*Another silence.*] Electra!

ELECTRA: Hurry up and go. Don't disappoint your fatherly old friend, who has bent down from Olympus to enlighten you. [*She stops abruptly, a look of wonder on her face.*] But—but what's come over you?

ORESTES [*slowly, in a tone he has not used till now*]: There is another way.

ELECTRA [*apprehensively*]: No, Philebus, don't be stubborn. You asked the gods for orders; now you have them.

ORESTES: Orders? What do you mean? Ah yes, the light round that big stone. But it's not for me, that light; from now on I'll take no one's orders, neither man's nor god's.

ELECTRA: You're speaking in riddles.

ORESTES: What a change has come on everything, and, oh, how far away you seem! Until now I felt something warm and living round me, like a friendly presence. That something has just died. What emptiness! What endless emptiness, as far as eye can reach! [*He takes some steps away from her.*] Night is coming on. The air is getting chilly, isn't it? But what was it—what was it that died just now?

ELECTRA: Philebus—

ORESTES: I say there is another path—*my* path. Can't you see it? It starts here and leads down to the city. I must go down—do you understand?—I must go

down into the depths, among you. For you are
living, all of you, at the bottom of a pit. [*He goes
up to* ELECTRA.] You are *my* sister, Electra, and that
city is *my* city. *My* sister. [*He takes her arm.*]

ELECTRA: Don't touch me. You're hurting me, fright-
ening me—and I'm *not* yours.

ORESTES: I know. Not yet. I'm still too—too light. I
must take a burden on my shoulders, a load of guilt
so heavy as to drag me down, right down into the
abyss of Argos.

ELECTRA: But what—what do you mean to do?

ORESTES: Wait. Give me time to say farewell to all the
lightness, the aery lightness that was mine. Let me
say good-by to my youth. There are evenings at
Corinth and at Athens, golden evenings full of songs
and scents and laughter; these I shall never know
again. And mornings, too, radiant with promise.
Good-by to them all, good-by. . . . Come, Electra,
look at our city. There it lies, rose-red in the sun,
buzzing with men and flies, drowsing its doom away
in the languor of a summer afternoon. It fends me
off with its high walls, red roofs, locked doors. And
yet it's mine for the taking; I've felt that since this
morning. You, too, Electra, are mine for the taking
—and I'll take you, too. I'll turn into an ax and hew
those walls asunder, I'll rip open the bellies of those
stolid houses and there will steam up from the gashes
a stench of rotting food and incense. I'll be an iron
wedge driven into the city, like a wedge rammed
into the heart of an oak tree.

ELECTRA: Oh, how you've changed! Your eyes have

◇◇◇

lost their glow; they're dull and smoldering. I'm sorry for that, Philebus; you were so gentle. But now you're talking like the Orestes of my dreams.

ORESTES: Listen! All those people quaking with fear in their dark rooms, with their dear departed round them—supposing I take over all their crimes. Supposing I set out to win the name of "guilt-stealer," and heap on myself all their remorse; that of the woman unfaithful to her husband, of the tradesman who let his mother die, of the usurer who bled his victims white? Surely, once I am plagued with all those pangs of conscience, innumerable as the flies of Argos—surely then I shall have earned the freedom of your city. Shall I not be as much at home within your red walls as the red-aproned butcher in his shop, among the carcasses of flayed sheep and cattle?

ELECTRA: So you wish to atone for us?

ORESTES: To atone? No, I said I'd house your penitence, but I did *not* say what I'd do with all those cackling fowls; maybe I'll wring their necks.

ELECTRA: And how can you take over our sense of guilt?

ORESTES: Why, all of you ask nothing better than to be rid of it. Only the King and Queen force you to nurse it in your foolish hearts.

ELECTRA: The King and Queen— Oh, Philebus!

ORESTES: The gods bear witness that I had no wish to shed their blood.

[*A long silence.*]

ELECTRA: You're too young, too weak.

ORESTES : Are you going to draw back—*now* ? Hide
me somewhere in the palace, and lead me tonight to
the royal bedchamber—and then you'll see if I am
too weak !

ELECTRA : Orestes !

ORESTES : Ah ! For the first time you've called me
Orestes.

ELECTRA : Yes. I know you now. You are indeed
Orestes. I didn't recognize you at first, I'd expected
somebody quite different. But this throbbing in my
blood, this sour taste on my lips—I've had them in
my dreams, and I know what they mean. So at last
you have come, Orestes, and your resolve is sure.
And here I am beside you—just as in my dreams—
on the brink of an act beyond all remedy. And I'm
frightened; that, too, was in my dreams. How long
I've waited for this moment, dreading and hoping
for it ! From now on, all the moments will link up,
like the cogs in a machine, and we shall never rest
again until they both are lying on their backs, with
faces like crushed mulberries. In a pool of blood. To
think it's you who are going to shed it, you with
those gentle eyes ! I'm sorry now, sorry that never
again I'll see that gentleness, never again see Philebus. Orestes, you are my elder brother, and head of
our house; fold me in your arms, protect me. Much
suffering, many perils lie ahead of both of us.

[ORESTES *takes her in his arms.* ZEUS *leaves his hiding-place and creeps out on tiptoe.*]

CURTAIN

SCENE II

The throne-room in the palace. An awe-inspiring, blood-smeared image of ZEUS *occupies a prominent position. The sun is setting.*

ELECTRA *enters : then beckons to* ORESTES *to follow her.*

ORESTES : Someone's coming.

[*He begins to draw his sword.*]

ELECTRA : It's the sentries on their rounds. Follow me. I know where to hide.

[*Two soldiers enter.*]

FIRST SOLDIER : I can't think what's come over the flies this evening. They're all crazy-like.

SECOND SOLDIER : They smell the Dead; that's why they're in such a state. Why, I daren't open my mouth to yawn for fear they all come teeming down my throat and start a round dance in my gullet. [ELECTRA *peeps from her hiding-place, then quickly withdraws her head.*] Hear that ? Something creaked yonder.

FIRST SOLDIER : Oh, it's only Agamemnon, sitting down on his throne.

SECOND SOLDIER : And the seat creaked when he planted his fat bottom on it ? No, it couldn't be that; a dead man's light as air.

FIRST SOLDIER : That goes for common folk like you and me. But a king, he's different. Mind you, Agamemnon always did himself proud at table. Why, he weighed two hundred pounds or more if he weighed one. It would be surprising if there wasn't some pounds left of all that flesh.

SECOND SOLDIER: So—so you think he's here, do you?

FIRST SOLDIER: Where else should he be? If I was a dead king and I had twenty-four hours' leave each year, you may be sure I'd spend them squatting on my throne, just to remind me of the high old times I had when I was His Almighty Majesty. And I'd stay put; I wouldn't run round pestering folks in their houses.

SECOND SOLDIER: Ah, wouldn't you? You say that because you're alive. But if you were dead, you'd be just as nasty as the others. [FIRST SOLDIER *smacks his face.*] Hey! What are you up to?

FIRST SOLDIER: I'm doing you a good turn. Look, I've killed seven of 'em, all at a go.

SECOND SOLDIER: Seven what? Seven dead 'uns?

FIRST SOLDIER: O' course not. *Flies.* Look, my hand's all bloody. [*He wipes it on his pants.*] Ugh, the filthy brutes!

SECOND SOLDIER: Pity you can't swot the lot of them while you're about it. The dead men, now—they don't do nothing, they know how to behave. If the flies were all killed off, we'd have some peace.

FIRST SOLDIER: Peace, you say? No, if I thought there were ghost-flies here as well, that'd be the last straw.

SECOND SOLDIER: Why?

FIRST SOLDIER: Don't you see? They die by millions every day, the little buzzers. Well, if all the flies that have died since last summer were set loose in the town, there'd be three hundred and sixty-five dead

◊◊

flies for every one that's here. The air'd be laced with flies, we'd breathe flies, eat flies, sweat flies; they'd be rolling down our throats in clusters and bunging up our lungs. . . . I wonder, now—maybe that's why there's such a funny smell in this room.

SECOND SOLDIER: No, no, it ain't that. They say our dead men have foul breaths, you know. And this room's not so big as it looks—a thousand square feet or so, I should say. Two or three dead men would be enough to foul the air.

FIRST SOLDIER: That's so. Fussing and fuming like they do.

SECOND SOLDIER: I tell you there's something amiss here. I heard a floor-board creak over there.

[*They go behind the throne to investigate.* ORESTES *and* ELECTRA *slip out on the left and tiptoe past the steps of the throne, returning to their hiding-place just as the soldiers emerge on the left.*]

FIRST SOLDIER: You see, there ain't nobody. It's only that old sod Agamemnon. Like as not, he's sitting on them cushions, straight as a poker. I shouldn't be surprised if he's watching you and me for want of anything else to do.

SECOND SOLDIER: Ay, and we'd better have a good look round, I ain't easy in my mind. These flies are something wicked, but it can't be helped.

FIRST SOLDIER: I wish I was back in the barracks. At least the dead folk there are old chums come back to visit us, just ordinary folk like us. But when I think that His Late Lamented Majesty is there, like as not counting the buttons missing on my tunic, well it makes me dithery, like when the general's doing an inspection.

[*Enter* ÆGISTHEUS *and* CLYTEMNESTRA, *followed by servants carrying lamps.*]

ÆGISTHEUS : Go, all of you.

[*Exeunt* SOLDIERS *and* SERVANTS.]

CLYTEMNESTRA : What is troubling you tonight?

ÆGISTHEUS : You saw what happened? Had I not played upon their fear, they'd have shaken off their remorse in the twinkling of an eye.

CLYTEMNESTRA : Is that all? Then be reassured. You will always find a way to freeze their courage when the need arises.

ÆGISTHEUS : I know. Oh, I'm only too skillful in the art of false pretense. [*A short silence.*] I am sorry I had to rebuke Electra.

CLYTEMNESTRA : Why? Because she is my daughter? It pleased you to so do, and all you do has my approval.

ÆGISTHEUS : Woman, it is not on your account that I regret it.

CLYTEMNESTRA : Then—why? You used not to have much love for Electra.

ÆGISTHEUS : I am tired. So tired. For fifteen years I have been upholding the remorse of a whole city, and my arms are aching with the strain. For fifteen years I have been dressing a part, playing the scaremonger, and the black of my robes has seeped through to my soul.

CLYTEMNESTRA : But, sire, I, too—

ÆGISTHEUS : I know, woman, I know. You are going

to tell me of your remorse. I wish I shared it. It fills out the void of your life. *I* have no remorse—and no man in Argos is sadder than I.

CLYTEMNESTRA: My sweet lord—

[*She goes up to him affectionately.*]

ÆGISTHEUS: Keep off, you whore! Are you not ashamed—under his eyes?

CLYTEMNESTRA: Under his eyes? Who can see us here?

ÆGISTHEUS: Why, the King. The Dead came forth this morning.

CLYTEMNESTRA: Sire, I beg you—the dead are underground and will not trouble us for many a long day. Have you forgotten it was you yourself who invented that fable to impress your people?

ÆGISTHEUS: That's so. Well, it only shows how tired I am, how sick at heart. Now leave me to my thoughts. [*Exit* CLYTEMNESTRA.] Have you in me, Lord Zeus, the king you wished for Argos? I come and go among my people, I speak in trumpet tones, I parade the terror of my frown, and all who see me cringe in an agony of repentance. But I—what am I but an empty shell? Some creature has devoured me unawares, gnawed out my inner self. And now, looking within, I see I am more dead than Agamemnon. Did I say I was sad? I lied. Neither sad nor gay is the desert—a boundless waste of sand under a burning waste of sky. Not sad, nor gay, but—sinister. Ah, I'd give my kingdom to be able to shed a tear.

[ZEUS *enters.*]

◇◇

ZEUS: That's right. Complain away! You're only a king, like every other king.

ÆGISTHEUS: Who are you? What are you doing here?

ZEUS: So you don't recognize me?

ÆGISTHEUS: Be gone, stranger, or I shall have you thrown out by my guards.

ZEUS: You don't recognize me? Still, you have seen me often enough, in dreams. It's true I looked more awe-inspiring. [*Flashes of lightning, a peal of thunder.* ZEUS *assumes an awe-inspiring air.*] And now do you know me?

ÆGISTHEUS: Zeus!

ZEUS: Good! [*Affable again, he goes up to the statue.*] So that's meant to be me? It's thus the Argives picture me at their prayers? Well, well, it isn't often that a god can study his likeness, face to face. [*A short silence.*] How hideous I am! They cannot like me much.

ÆGISTHEUS: They fear you.

ZEUS: Excellent! I've no use for love. Do you, Ægistheus, love me?

ÆGISTHEUS: What do you want of me? Have I not paid heavily enough?

ZEUS: Never enough.

ÆGISTHEUS: But it's killing me, the task I have undertaken.

ZEUS: Come now! Don't exaggerate! Your health is none too bad; you're fat. Mind, I'm not reproaching you. It's good, royal fat, yellow as tallow—just as it should be. You're built to live another twenty years.

ÆGISTHEUS: Another twenty years!

ZEUS : Would you rather die?

ÆGISTHEUS : Yes.

ZEUS : So, if anyone came here now, with a drawn sword, would you bare your breast to him?

ÆGISTHEUS : I—I cannot say.

ZEUS : Now mark my words. If you let yourself be slaughtered like a dumb ox, your doom will be exemplary. You shall be King in hell for all eternity. That's what I came here to tell you.

ÆGISTHEUS : Is someone planning to kill me?

ZEUS : So it seems.

ÆGISTHEUS : Electra?

ZEUS : Not only Electra.

ÆGISTHEUS : Who?

ZEUS : Orestes.

ÆGISTHEUS : Oh! . . . Well, that's in the natural order of things, no doubt. What can I do against it?

ZEUS [*mimicking his tone*] : What can I do? [*Imperiously*] Bid your men arrest a young stranger going under the name of Philebus. Have him and Electra thrown into a dungeon—and if you leave them there to rot, I'll think no worse of you. Well, what are you waiting for? Call your men.

ÆGISTHEUS : No.

ZEUS : Be good enough to tell me why that no.

ÆGISTHEUS : I am tired.

ZEUS : Don't stare at the ground. Raise your big, bloodshot eyes and look at me. That's better. Yes, you're majestically stupid, like a horse; a kingly fool. But yours is not the stubbornness that vexes me; rather, it will add a spice to your surrender. For I know you will obey me in the end.

ÆGISTHEUS: I tell you I refuse to fall in with your plans. I have done so far too often.

ZEUS: That's right. Show your mettle! Resist! Resist! Ah, how I cherish souls like yours! Your eyes flash, you clench your fists, you fling refusal in the teeth of Zeus. None the less, my little rebel, my restive little horse, no sooner had I warned you than your heart said yes. Of course you'll obey. Do you think I leave Olympus without good reason? I wished to warn you of this crime because it is my will to avert it.

ÆGISTHEUS: To warn me! How strange!

ZEUS: Why "strange"? Surely it's natural enough. Your life's in danger and I want to save it.

ÆGISTHEUS: Who asked you to save it? What about Agamemnon? Did you warn *him*? And yet *he* wished to live.

ZEUS: O miserable man, what base ingratitude! You are dearer to me than Agamemnon, and when I prove this, you complain!

ÆGISTHEUS: Dearer than Agamemnon? I? No, it's Orestes whom you cherish. You allowed me to work my doom, you let me rush in, ax in hand, to King Agamemnon's bath—and no doubt you watched from high Olympus, licking your lips at the thought of another damned soul to gloat over. But today you are protecting young Orestes against himself; and I, whom you egged on to kill his father—you have chosen me to restrain the young man's hand. I was a poor creature, just qualified for murder; but for Orestes, it seems, you have higher destinies in view.

ZEUS: What strange jealousy is this! But have no fear; I love him no more than I love you. I love nobody.

ÆGISTHEUS: Then see what you have made of me, unjust god that you are. And tell me this. If today you hinder the crime Orestes has in mind, why did you permit mine of fifteen years ago?

ZEUS: All crimes do not displease me equally. And now, Ægistheus, I shall speak to you frankly, as one king to another. The first crime was mine; I committed it when I made man mortal. Once I had done that, what was left for you, poor human murderers, to do? To kill your victims? But they already had the seed of death in them; all you could do was to hasten its fruition by a year or two. Do you know what would have befallen Agamemnon if you had not killed him? Three months later he'd have died of apoplexy in a pretty slave-girl's arms. But your crime served my ends.

ÆGISTHEUS: What ends? For fifteen years I have been atoning for it—and you say it served your ends!

ZEUS: Exactly. It's because you are atoning for it that it served my ends. I like crimes that *pay*. I like yours because it was a clumsy, boorish murder, a crime that did not know itself, a crime in the antique mode, more like a cataclysm than an act of man. Not for one moment did you defy me. You struck in a frenzy of fear and rage. And then, when your frenzy had died down, you looked back on the deed with loathing and disowned it. Yet what a profit I have made on it! For one dead man, twenty thousand living men wallowing in penitence. Yes, it was a good bargain I struck that day.

ÆGISTHEUS: I see what lies behind your words. Orestes will have no remorse.

ZEUS: Not a trace of it. At this moment he is thinking out his plan, coolly, methodically, cheerfully. What good to me is a carefree murder, a shameless, sedate crime, that lies light as thistledown on the murderer's conscience? No, I won't allow it. Ah, how I loathe the crimes of this new generation; thankless and sterile as the wind! Yes, that nice-minded young man will kill you as he'd kill a chicken; he'll go away with red hands and a clean heart. In your place I should feel humiliated. So—call your men!

ÆGISTHEUS: Again I tell you, I will *not*. The crime that is being hatched displeases you enough for me to welcome it.

ZEUS: Ægistheus, you are a king, and it's to your sense of kingship I appeal, for you enjoy wielding the scepter.

ÆGISTHEUS: Continue.

ZEUS: You may hate me, but we are akin; I made you in my image. A king is a god on earth, glorious and terrifying as a god.

ÆGISTHEUS: You, terrifying?

ZEUS: Look at me. [*A long silence.*] I told you you were made in my image. Each keeps order; you in Argos, I in heaven and on earth—and you and I harbor the same dark secret in our hearts.

ÆGISTHEUS: I have no secret.

ZEUS: You have. The same as mine. The bane of gods and kings. The bitterness of knowing men are free. Yes, Ægistheus, they are free. But your subjects do not know it, and you do.

ÆGISTHEUS: Why, yes. If they knew it, they'd send my palace up in flames. For fifteen years I've been playing a part to mask their power from them.

ZEUS: So you see we are alike.

ÆGISTHEUS: Alike? A god likening himself to me— what freak of irony is this? Since I came to the throne, all I said, all my acts, have been aimed at building up an image of myself. I wish each of my subjects to keep that image in the foreground of his mind, and to feel, even when alone, that my eyes are on him, severely judging his most private thoughts. But I have been trapped in my own net. I have come to see myself only as they see me. I peer into the dark pit of their souls, and there, deep down, I see the image that I have built up. I shudder, but I cannot take my eyes off it. Almighty Zeus, who am I? Am I anything more than the dread that others have of me?

ZEUS: And I—who do you think *I* am? [*Points to the statue.*] I, too, have my image, and do you suppose it doesn't fill me with confusion? For a hundred thousand years I have been dancing a slow, dark ritual dance before men's eyes. Their eyes are so intent on me that they forget to look into themselves. If I forgot myself for a single moment, if I let their eyes turn away—

ÆGISTHEUS: Yes?

ZEUS: Enough. That is *my* business. Ægistheus, I know that you are weary of it all; but why complain? You'll die one day—but I shall not. So long as there are men on earth, I am doomed to go on dancing before them.

ÆGISTHEUS: Alas! But who has doomed us?

ZEUS: No one but ourselves. For we have the same passion. You, Ægistheus, have, like me, a passion for order.

ÆGISTHEUS: For order? That is so. It was for the sake of order that I wooed Clytemnestra, for order that I killed my King; I wished that order should prevail, and that it should prevail through me. I have lived without love, without hope, even without lust. But I have kept order. Yes, I have kept good order in my kingdom. That has been my ruling passion; a godlike passion, but how terrible!

ZEUS: We could have no other, you and I; I am God, and you were born to be a king.

ÆGISTHEUS: Ay, more's the pity!

ZEUS: Ægistheus, my creature and my mortal brother, in the name of this good order that we serve, both you and I, I ask you—nay, I command you—to lay hands on Orestes and his sister.

ÆGISTHEUS: Are they so dangerous?

ZEUS: Orestes knows that he is free.

ÆGISTHEUS [*eagerly*]: He knows he's free? Then, to lay hands on him, to put him in irons, is not enough. A free man in a city acts like a plague-spot. He will infect my whole kingdom and bring my work to

◇◇◇

nothing. Almighty Zeus, why stay your hand? Why
not fell him with a thunderbolt?

ZEUS [*slowly*]: Fell him with a thunderbolt? [*A
pause. Then, in a muffled voice*] Ægistheus, the
gods have another secret.

ÆGISTHEUS: Yes?

ZEUS: Once freedom lights its beacon in a man's heart,
the gods are powerless against him. It's a matter between man and man, and it is for other men, and
for them only, to let him go his gait, or to throttle
him.

ÆGISTHEUS [*observing him closely*]: To throttle him?
Be it so. Well, I shall do your will, no doubt. But
say no more, and stay here no longer—I could not
bear it.

[*As* ZEUS *departs,* ELECTRA *leaps forward and rushes
to the door.* ORESTES *comes forward.*]

ELECTRA: Strike him down! Don't give him time to
call for help. I'll bar the door.

ÆGISTHEUS: So you, young man, are Orestes?

ORESTES: Defend yourself.

ÆGISTHEUS: I shall not defend myself. It's too late for
me to call for help, and I am glad it is too late. No,
I shall not resist. I *wish* you to kill me.

ORESTES: Good. Little I care how it is done. . . . So I
am to be a murderer.

[ORESTES *strikes him with his sword.*]

ÆGISTHEUS [*tottering*]: Ah! You struck well, Orestes.
[*He clings to* ORESTES.] Let me look at you. Is it true
you feel no remorse?

ORESTES : Remorse? Why should I feel remorse? I am only doing what is right.

ÆGISTHEUS : What is right is the will of God. You were hidden here and you heard the words of Zeus.

ORESTES : What do I care for Zeus? Justice is a matter between men, and I need no god to teach me it. It's right to stamp you out, like the foul brute you are, and to free the people of Argos from your evil influence. It is right to restore to them their sense of human dignity.

ÆGISTHEUS [*groaning*] : Pain! What agony!

ELECTRA : Look! Look! He's swaying; his face has gone quite gray. What an ugly sight's a dying man!

ORESTES : Keep silent! Let him carry with him to the grave no other memory than the memory of our joy.

ÆGISTHEUS : My curse on you both!

ORESTES : Won't you have done with dying?

[*He strikes again. ÆGISTHEUS falls.*]

ÆGISTHEUS : Beware of the flies, Orestes, beware of the flies. All is not over.

[*Dies.*]

ORESTES [*giving the body a kick*] : For him, anyhow, all is over. Now lead me to the Queen's room.

ELECTRA : Orestes!

ORESTES : What?

ELECTRA : She—she can do us no more harm.

ORESTES : What of it? What has come over you? This is not how you spoke a little while ago.

ELECTRA : Orestes! You, too, have changed. I hardly recognize you.

◇◇◇

ORESTES : Very well. I'll go alone.

[*Exit.*]

ELECTRA [*to herself*] : Will she scream ? [*Silence. She is listening.*] He's walking down the passage. When he opens the fourth door— Oh, I wanted this to happen. And I—I want it now, I *must* want it. [*She looks at* ÆGISTHEUS.] That one—yes, he's dead. So *this* is what I wanted. I didn't realize how it would be. [*She comes closer to the body.*] A hundred times I've seen him, in my dreams, lying just where he is now, with a sword through his heart. His eyes were closed, he seemed asleep. How I hated him, what joy I got from hating him ! But he doesn't seem asleep; his eyes are open, staring up at me. He is dead, and my hatred is dead, too. And I'm standing here, waiting, waiting. That woman is still alive, she's in her bedroom, and presently she'll be screaming. Screaming like an animal in pain. No, I can't bear those eyes any longer. [*Kneeling, she lays a mantle over the King's face.*] What was it, then, I wanted ? What ? [*A short silence.* CLYTEMNESTRA *screams.*] He's struck her. She was our mother— and he's struck her. [*She rises to her feet.*] It's done; my enemies are dead. For years and years I've reveled in the thought of this, and, now it's happened, my heart is like a lump of ice. Was I lying to myself all those years ? No, that's not true, it can't be true. I'm not a coward. Only a moment ago I wanted it, and I haven't changed. I'm glad, glad, to see that swine lying at my feet. [*She jerks the mantle off the dead King's face.*] Those dead-fish eyes goggling up at nothing—why should they trouble me? That's how I wanted to see them, dead and staring, and I'm glad, glad— [CLYTEMNESTRA's *screams are weakening*.] Let her scream! Make her scream, Orestes. I want her to suffer. [*The screams cease.*] Oh joy, joy! I'm weeping for joy; my enemies are dead, my father is avenged.

[ORESTES *returns, his sword dripping blood.* ELECTRA *runs to him and flings herself into his arms.*]

ELECTRA: Orestes! . . . Oh! . . .

ORESTES: You're frightened. Why?

ELECTRA: I'm not frightened. I'm drunk. Drunk with joy. What did she say? Did she beg for mercy long?

ORESTES: Electra, I shall not repent of what I have done, but I think fit not to speak of it. There are some memories one does not share. It is enough for you to know she's dead.

ELECTRA: Did she die cursing us? That's all I want you to tell me. Did she curse us?

ORESTES: Yes. She died cursing us.

ELECTRA: Take me in your arms, beloved, and press me to your breast. How dark the night is! I never knew such darkness; those torches have no effect on it. . . . Do you love me?

ORESTES: It is not night; a new day is dawning. We are free, Electra. I feel as if I'd brought you into life and I, too, had just been born. Yes, I love you, and you belong to me. Only yesterday I was empty-handed, and today I have *you*. Ours is a double tie of blood; we two come of the same race and we two have shed blood.

◇◇

ELECTRA : Let go your sword. Give me that hand, your strong right hand. [*She clasps and kisses it.*] Your fingers are short and square, made to grasp and hold. Dear hand ! It's whiter than mine. But how heavy it became to strike down our father's murderers ! Wait ! [*She takes a torch and holds it near* ORESTES.] I must light up your face; it's getting so dark that I can hardly see you. And I *must* see you; when I stop seeing you, I'm afraid of you. I daren't take my eyes off you. I must tell myself again and again that I love you. But—how strange you look !

ORESTES : I am free, Electra. Freedom has crashed down on me like a thunderbolt.

ELECTRA : Free ? But I—I don't feel free. And you— can you undo what has been done ? Something has happened and we are no longer free to blot it out. Can you prevent our being the murderers of our mother—for all time ?

ORESTES : Do you think I'd wish to prevent it ? I have done *my* deed, Electra, and that deed was good. I shall bear it on my shoulders as a carrier at a ferry carries the traveler to the farther bank. And when I have brought it to the farther bank I shall take stock of it. The heavier it is to carry, the better pleased I shall be; for that burden is my freedom. Only yester- day I walked the earth haphazard; thousands of roads I tramped that brought me nowhere, for they were other men's roads. Yes, I tried them all; the haulers' tracks along the riverside, the mule-paths in the mountains, and the broad, flagged highways of

the charioteers. But none of these was mine. Today
I have one path only, and heaven knows where it
leads. But it is *my* path. . . . What is it, Electra?

ELECTRA: I can't see you any more. Those torches
give no light. I hear your voice, but it hurts me, it
cuts like a knife. Will it always be as dark as this—
always, even in the daytime? . . . Oh, Orestes!
There they are!

ORESTES: Who?

ELECTRA: There they are! Where have they come
from? They're hanging from the ceiling like clusters
of black grapes; the walls are alive with them; they're
swirling down across the torchlight and it's their
shadows that are hiding your face from me.

ORESTES: The flies—

ELECTRA: Listen! The sound of their wings is like a
roaring furnace. They're all round us, Orestes,
watching, biding their time. Presently they'll swoop
down on us and I shall feel thousands of tiny clammy
feet crawling over me. Oh, look! They're growing
bigger, bigger; now they're as big as bees. We'll
never escape them, they'll follow us everywhere in a
dense cloud. Oh God, now I can see their eyes, millions of beady eyes all staring at us!

ORESTES: What do the flies matter to us?

ELECTRA: They're the Furies, Orestes, the goddesses of
remorse.

VOICES [*from behind the door*]: Open! Open! . . .
If you don't, we'll smash the door in.
[*Heavy thuds. They are battering at the door.*]

ORESTES : Clytemnestra's cries must have brought them here. Come! Lead me to Apollo's shrine. We will spend the night there, sheltered from men and flies. And tomorrow I shall speak to my people.

CURTAIN

A C T   I I I

*The temple of Apollo. Twilight. A statue of Apollo in
the center of the stage.* ELECTRA *and* ORESTES *are
sleeping at the foot of the statue, their arms clasped
round its legs. The* FURIES *ring them round; they
sleep standing, like cranes.*
At the back is a huge bronze door.

FIRST FURY [*stretching herself*] : Aaaah! I slept the
night out standing, stiff with rage, and my sleep was
glorious with angry dreams. Ah, how lovely is the
flower of anger, the red flower in my heart! [*She
circles round* ORESTES *and* ELECTRA.] Still sleeping.
How white and soft they are! I'll roll on their
breasts and bellies, like a torrent over stones. And I
shall polish hour by hour their tender flesh; rub it,
scour it, wear it to the bone. [*She comes a few steps
forward.*] Oh clear, bright dawn of hate! A superb
awakening. They're sleeping, sweating, a smell of
fever rises from them. But I am awake; cool and
hard and gemlike. My soul is adamant—and I feel
my sanctity.

ELECTRA [*sighing in her sleep*] : No! No!

FIRST FURY : She's sighing. Wait, my pretty one, wait
till you feel our teeth. Soon you'll be screaming with
the agony of our caresses. I'll woo you like a man,
for you're my bride, and you shall feel my love
crushing your life out. You, Electra, are more beau-

◇◇◇

tiful than I; but you'll see how my kisses age you. Within six months I'll have you raddled like an old hag; but I stay young forever. [*She bends over* ORESTES *and* ELECTRA.] Ah, this lovely human carrion, what a tasty meal we have in store! As I gaze down at them and breathe their breath, I choke with rage. Nothing is sweeter, nothing, than to feel a dawn of hatred spreading like quickfire in one's veins; teeth and talons ready for their task. Hatred is flooding through me, welling up in my breasts like milk. Awake, sisters, awake! The day has come.

SECOND FURY: I dreamt I was biting them.

FIRST FURY: Be patient. Today they are protected by a god, but soon hunger and thirst will drive them out of sanctuary. And then you shall bite them to your heart's content.

THIRD FURY: Aaah! How I want to claw them!

FIRST FURY: Your turn will come. In a little while your iron talons will be ribboning the flesh of those young criminals with angry red. Come closer, sisters, come and look at them.

A FURY: How young they are!

ANOTHER FURY: And how beautiful!

FIRST FURY: Yes, we are favored. Only too often criminals are old and ugly. Too seldom do we have the joy, the exquisite delight, of ruining what's beautiful.

THE FURIES: Heiah! Heiahah!

THIRD FURY: Orestes is almost a child. I shall mother him, oh so tenderly, with my hatred; I shall take his pale head on my knees and stroke his hair.

FIRST FURY : And then?

THIRD FURY : Then, when he least expects it, I shall dig
these two fingers into his eyes.

[*All laugh.*]

FIRST FURY : See, they're stretching, sighing, on the
brink of waking. And now, my sisters, flies my sisters, let's sing the sinners from their sleep.

THE FURIES [*together*] : Bzz. Bzz. Bzz. Bzz.

We shall settle on your rotten hearts like flies on
butter;

Rotten hearts, juicy, luscious hearts.

Like bees we'll suck the pus and matter from your
hearts,

And we'll turn it into honey, rich, green honey.

What love could ravish us as hatred does?

Bzz. Bzz. Bzz. Bzz.

We shall be the staring eyes of the houses,

The growls of the kenneled mastiff baring his fangs
as you go by,

A drone of wings pulsing in high air,

Sounds of the forest,

Whistlings, whinings, creakings, hissings, howlings,

We shall be the darkness,

The clotted darkness of your souls.

Bzz. Bzz. Bzz. Bzz.

Heiah, heiah, heiahah !

Bzz. Bzz. Bzz. Bzz.

We are the flies, the suckers of pus,

We shall have open house with you,

We shall gather our food from your mouths,

And our light from the depths of your eyes.

All your life we will be with you,
Until we make you over to the worms.
[*They dance.*]

ELECTRA [*still half asleep*] : Was someone speaking?
Who—who are you?

THE FURIES : Bzz. Bzz. Bzz.

ELECTRA.: Ah, yes. There you are. Well? Have we
really killed them?

ORESTES [*waking*] : Electra!

ELECTRA : You, who are you? Ah, yes. Orestes. Go
away.

ORESTES : But—what's wrong, Electra?

ELECTRA : You frighten me. I had a dream. I saw our
mother lying on her back. Blood was pouring from
her, gushing under the doors. A dream. . . . Feel
my hands. They're icy. No, don't. Don't touch me.
Did she really bleed much?

ORESTES : Don't!

ELECTRA [*waking up completely*] : Let me look at you.
You killed them. It was you, you who killed them.
You are here beside me, you have just waked up,
there's nothing written on your face, no brand. . . .
And yet you killed them.

ORESTES : Why, yes. I killed them. [*A short silence.*]
You, too, make me afraid. Yesterday you were so
beautiful. And now you look as if some wild beast
had clawed your face.

ELECTRA : No beast. Your crime. It's tearing off my
cheeks and eyelids; I feel as if my eyes and teeth
were naked. . . . But what are those creatures?

ORESTES : Take no notice of them. They can do you no
harm.

FIRST FURY: No harm? Let her dare to come among us and you'll see if we can do no harm!

ORESTES: Keep quiet. Back to your kennel, bitches! [*The* FURIES *growl.*] Is it possible that the girl who only yesterday was dancing in a white dress on the temple steps—is it possible you were that girl?

ELECTRA: I've grown old. In a single night.

ORESTES: You have not lost your beauty, but—Where, now, have I seen dead eyes like those? Electra— you are like *her*. Like Clytemnestra. What use, then, was it killing her? When I see my crime in those eyes, it revolts me.

FIRST FURY: That is because *you* revolt *her*.

ORESTES: Is that true, Electra? Do I revolt you?

ELECTRA: Oh, let me be!

FIRST FURY: Well? Can you still have any doubt? How should she not hate you? She lived in peace, dreaming her dreams; and then you came, bringing murder and impiety upon her. So now she has to share your guilt and hug that pedestal, the only scrap of earth remaining to her.

ORESTES: Do not listen.

FIRST FURY: Away! Away! Make him go, Electra; don't let him touch you! He's a butcher. He reeks of fresh, warm blood. He used the poor old woman very foully, you know; he killed her piecemeal.

ELECTRA: Oh no! That's a lie, surely?

FIRST FURY: You can believe me; I was there all the time, buzzing in the air around them.

ELECTRA: So he struck her several times?

FIRST FURY: Ten times at least. And each time the

◇◇

sword squelched in the wound. She tried to shield her face and belly with her hands, and he carved her hands to ribbons.

ELECTRA: So it wasn't a quick death. Did she suffer much?

ORESTES: Put your fingers in your ears, do not look at them, and, above all, ask no questions. If you question them, you're lost.

FIRST FURY: Yes, she suffered—horribly.

ELECTRA [*covering her face with her hands*]: Oh!

ORESTES: She wants to part us, she is building up a wall of solitude around you. But beware; once you are alone, alone and helpless, they will fling themselves upon you. Electra, we planned this crime together and we should bear its brunt together.

ELECTRA: You dare to say I planned it with you?

ORESTES: Can you deny it?

ELECTRA: Of course I deny it. Wait! Well, perhaps— in a way. . . . Oh, I don't know. I dreamt the crime, but you carried it out, you murdered your own mother.

THE FURIES [*shrieking and laughing*]: Murderer! Murderer! Butcher!

ORESTES: Electra, behind that door is the outside world. A world of dawn. Out there the sun is rising, lighting up the roads. Soon we shall leave this place, we shall walk those sunlit roads, and these hags of darkness will lose their power. The sunbeams will cut through them like swords.

ELECTRA: The sun—

FIRST FURY: You will never see the sun again, Electra.

We shall mass between you and the sun like a swarm of locusts; you will carry darkness round your head wherever you go.

ELECTRA : Oh, let me be ! Stop torturing me !

ORESTES : It's your weakness gives them their strength. Mark how they dare not speak to me. A nameless horror has descended on you, keeping us apart. And yet why should this be ? What have you lived through that I have not shared ? Do you imagine that my mother's cries will ever cease ringing in my ears ? Or that my eyes will ever cease to see her great sad eyes, lakes of lambent darkness in the pallor of her face ? And the anguish that consumes you—do you think it will ever cease ravaging my heart ? But what matter ? I am free. Beyond anguish, beyond remorse. Free. And at one with myself. No, you must not loathe yourself, Electra. Give me your hand. I shall never forsake you.

ELECTRA : Let go of my hand ! Those hell-hounds frighten me, but you frighten me more.

FIRST FURY : You see ! You see ! . . . That's quite true, little doll; you're less afraid of us than of that man. Because you need us, Electra. You are our child, our little girl. You need our nails to score your skin, our teeth to bite your breast, and all our savage love to save you from your hatred of yourself. Only the suffering of your body can take your mind off your suffering soul. So come and let us hurt you. You have only those two steps to come down, and we will take you in our arms. And when our kisses

◇◇◇

sear your tender flesh, you'll forget all in the cleansing fires of pain.

THE FURIES : Come down to us ! Come down !

[*Slowly they dance round her, weaving their spell.* ELECTRA *rises to her feet.*]

ORESTES [*gripping her arm*] : No, no, for pity's sake. Don't go to them. Once they get you, all is lost.

ELECTRA [*freeing herself violently*] : Let go ! Oh, how I hate you ! [*She goes down the steps, and the* FURIES *fling themselves on her.*] Help !

[ZEUS *enters.*]

ZEUS : Kennel up !

FIRST FURY : The master !

[*The* FURIES *slink off reluctantly, leaving* ELECTRA *lying on the ground.*]

ZEUS : Poor children. [*He goes up to* ELECTRA.] So to this you've come, unhappy pair ? My heart is torn between anger and compassion. Get up, Electra. So long as I am here, my Furies will not hurt you. [*He helps her to rise and gazes at her face.*] Ah, what a cruel change ! In a night, a single night, all the wild-rose bloom has left your cheeks. In one night your body has gone to ruin, lungs, gall, and liver all burnt out. The pride of headstrong youth—see what it has brought you to, poor child.

ORESTES : Stop talking in that tone, fellow. It is unbecoming for the king of the gods.

ZEUS : And you, my lad, drop that haughty tone. It's unbecoming for a criminal atoning for his crime.

ORESTES : I am no criminal, and you have no power

to make me atone for an act I don't regard as a crime.

ZEUS: So you may think, but wait awhile. I shall cure you of that error before long.

ORESTES: Torture me to your heart's content; I regret nothing.

ZEUS: Not even the doom you have brought upon your sister?

ORESTES: Not even that.

ZEUS: Do you hear, Electra? And this man professed to love you!

ORESTES: She is dearer to me than life. But her suffering comes from within, and only she can rid herself of it. For she is free.

ZEUS: And you? You, too, are free, no doubt?

ORESTES: Yes, and well you know it.

ZEUS: A pity you can't see yourself as you are now, you fool, for all your boasting! What a heroic figure you cut there, cowering between the legs of a protecting god, with a pack of hungry vixen keeping guard on you! If *you* can brag of freedom, why not praise the freedom of a prisoner languishing in fetters, or a slave nailed to the cross?

ORESTES: Certainly. Why not?

ZEUS: Take care. You play the braggart now because Apollo is protecting you. But Apollo is my most obedient servant. I have but to lift a finger and he will abandon you.

ORESTES: Then do so. Lift a finger, lift your whole hand while you are about it.

◇◇◇

ZEUS : No, that is not my way. Haven't I told you that I take no pleasure in punishment? I have come to save you both.

ELECTRA : To save us? No, it is too cruel to make sport of us. You are the lord of vengeance and of death, but, god though you are, you have no right to delude your victims with false hopes.

ZEUS : Within a quarter of an hour you can be outside that door.

ELECTRA : Safe and sound?

ZEUS : You have my word for it.

ELECTRA : And what do you want from me in return?

ZEUS : Nothing, my child. Nothing.

ELECTRA : Nothing? Did I hear right? Then you are a kind god, a lovable god.

ZEUS : Or next to nothing. A mere trifle. What you can give most easily—a little penitence.

ORESTES : Take care, Electra. That trifle will weigh like a millstone on your soul.

ZEUS [*to* ELECTRA] : Don't listen to him. Answer me, instead. Why hesitate to disavow that crime? It was committed by someone else; one could hardly say even that you were his accomplice.

ORESTES : Electra! Are you going to go back on fifteen years of hope and hatred?

ZEUS : What has she to go back on? Never did she really wish that impious deed to be accomplished.

ELECTRA : If only that were true!

ZEUS : Come now! Surely you can trust my word. Do I not read in men's hearts?

◇◇◇

ELECTRA [*incredulously*] : And you read in mine that I never really desired that crime ? Though for fifteen years I dreamt of murder and revenge ?

ZEUS : Bah ! I know you nursed bloodthirsty dreams— but there was a sort of innocence about them. They made you forget your servitude, they healed your wounded pride. But you never really thought of making them come true. Well, am I mistaken ?

ELECTRA : Ah, Zeus, dear Zeus, how I long to think you are not mistaken !

ZEUS : You're a little girl, Electra. A mere child. Most little girls dream of becoming the richest or the love-liest woman on earth. But you were haunted by the cruel destiny of your race, you dreamt of becoming the saddest, most criminal of women. You never willed to do evil; you willed your own misfortune. At an age when most children are playing hopscotch or with their dolls, you, poor child, who had no friends or toys, you toyed with dreams of murder, because that's a game to play alone.

ELECTRA : Yes, yes ! I'm beginning to understand.

ORESTES : Listen, Electra ! It's *now* you are bringing guilt upon you. For who except yourself can know what you really wanted ? Will you let another de-cide that for you ? Why distort a past that can no longer stand up for itself ? And why disown the fire-brand that you were, that glorious young goddess, vivid with hatred, that I loved so much ? Can't you see this cruel god is fooling you ?

ZEUS : No, Electra, I'm not fooling you. And now hear

what I offer. If you repudiate your crime, I'll see that you two occupy the throne of Argos.

ORESTES: Taking the places of our victims?

ZEUS: How else?

ORESTES: And I shall put on the royal robe, still warm from the dead King's wearing?

ZEUS: That or another. What can it matter?

ORESTES: Nothing of course—provided that it's black.

ZEUS: Are you not in mourning?

ORESTES: Yes, I was forgetting; in mourning for my mother. And my subjects—must I have them, too, wear black?

ZEUS: They wear it already.

ORESTES: True. We can give them time to wear out their old clothes. . . . Well, Electra, have you understood? If you shed some tears, you'll be given Clytemnestra's shifts and petticoats—those dirty, stinking ones you had to wash for fifteen years. And the part she played is yours for the asking. Now that you have come to look so much like her, you will play the part superbly; everyone will take you for your mother. But I—I fear I am more squeamish— I refuse to wear the breeches of the clown I killed.

ZEUS: You talk big, my boy. You butchered a defenseless man and an old woman who begged for mercy. But, to hear you speak, one would think you'd bravely fought, one against a crowd, and were the savior of your city.

ORESTES: Perhaps I was.

ZEUS: You a savior! Do you know what's afoot behind that door? All the good folk of Argos are waiting there. Waiting to greet you with stones and pikes and pitchforks. Oh, they are very grateful to their savior! . . . You are lonely as a leper.

ORESTES: Yes.

ZEUS: So you take pride in being an outcast, do you? But the solitude you're doomed to, most cowardly of murderers, is the solitude of scorn and loathing.

ORESTES: The most cowardly of murderers is he who feels remorse.

ZEUS: Orestes, I created you, and I created all things. Now see! [*The walls of the temple draw apart, revealing the firmament, spangled with wheeling stars.* ZEUS *is standing in the background. His voice becomes huge—amplified by loud-speakers—but his form is shadowy.*] See those planets wheeling on their appointed ways, never swerving, never clashing. It was I who ordained their courses, according to the law of justice. Hear the music of the spheres, that vast, mineral hymn of praise, sounding and resounding to the limits of the firmament. [*Sounds of music.*] It is my work that living things increase and multiply, each according to his kind. I have ordained that man shall always beget man, and dog give birth to dog. It is my work that the tides with their innumerable tongues creep up to lap the sand and draw back at the appointed hour. I make the plants grow, and my breath fans round the earth the yellow clouds of pollen. You are not in your own home, intruder; you are a foreign body in the world, like a splinter in flesh, or a poacher in his lordship's forest. For the world is good; I made it according to my

◇◇◇

will, and I am Goodness. But you, Orestes, you have done evil, the very rocks and stones cry out against you. The Good is everywhere, it is the coolness of the wellspring, the pith of the reed, the grain of flint, the weight of stone. Yes, you will find it even in the heart of fire and light; even your own body plays you false, for it abides perforce by my law. Good is everywhere, in you and about you; sweeping through you like a scythe, crushing you like a mountain. Like an ocean it buoys you up and rocks you to and fro, and it enabled the success of your evil plan, for it was in the brightness of the torches, the temper of your blade, the strength of your right arm. And that of which you are so vain, the Evil that you think is your creation, what is it but a reflection in a mocking mirror, a phantom thing that would have no being but for Goodness. No, Orestes, return to your saner self; the universe refutes you, you are a mite in the scheme of things. Return to Nature, Nature's thankless son. Know your sin, abhor it, and tear it from you as one tears out a rotten, noisome tooth. Or else—beware lest the very seas shrink back at your approach, springs dry up when you pass by, stones and rocks roll from your path, and the earth crumbles under your feet.

ORESTES: Let it crumble! Let the rocks revile me, and flowers wilt at my coming. Your whole universe is not enough to prove me wrong. You are the king of gods, king of stones and stars, king of the waves of the sea. But you are not the king of man.

[*The walls draw together.* ZEUS *comes into view,*

◇◇

tired and dejected, and he now speaks in his normal voice.]

ZEUS: Impudent spawn! So I am not your king? Who, then, made you?

ORESTES: You. But you blundered; you should not have made me free.

ZEUS: I gave you freedom so that you might serve me.

ORESTES: Perhaps. But now it has turned against its giver. And neither you nor I can undo what has been done.

ZEUS: Ah, at last! So this is your excuse?

ORESTES: I am not excusing myself.

ZEUS: No? Let me tell you it sounds much like an excuse, this freedom whose slave you claim to be.

ORESTES: Neither slave nor master. I *am* my freedom. No sooner had you created me than I ceased to be yours.

ELECTRA: Oh, Orestes! By all you hold most holy, by our father's memory, I beg you do not add blasphemy to your crime!

ZEUS: Mark her words, young man. And hope no more to win her back by arguments like these. Such language is somewhat new to her ears—and somewhat shocking.

ORESTES: To my ears, too. And to my lungs, which breathe the words, and to my tongue, which shapes them. In fact, I can hardly understand myself. Only yesterday you were still a veil on my eyes, a clot of wax in my ears; yesterday, indeed, I had an excuse. *You* were my excuse for being alive, for you had put me in the world to fulfill your purpose, and the world was an old pandar prating to me about your goodness, day in, day out. And then you forsook me.

ZEUS: *I* forsook you? How?

ORESTES: Yesterday, when I was with Electra, I felt at one with Nature, this Nature of your making. It sang the praises of the Good—*your* Good—in siren tones, and lavished intimations. To lull me into gentleness, the fierce light mellowed and grew tender as a lover's eyes. And, to teach me the forgiveness of offenses, the sky grew bland as a pardoner's face. Obedient to your will, my youth rose up before me and pleaded with me like a girl who fears her lover will forsake her. That was the last time, the last, I saw my youth. Suddenly, out of the blue, freedom crashed down on me and swept me off my feet. Nature sprang back, my youth went with the wind, and I knew myself alone, utterly alone in the midst of this well-meaning little universe of yours. I was like a man who's lost his shadow. And there was nothing left in heaven, no right or wrong, nor anyone to give me orders.

ZEUS: What of it? Do you want me to admire a scabby sheep that has to be kept apart; or the leper mewed in a lazar-house? Remember, Orestes, you once were of my flock, you fed in my pastures among my sheep. Your vaunted freedom isolates you from the fold; it means exile.

ORESTES: Yes, exile.

ZEUS: But the disease can't be deeply rooted yet; it began only yesterday. Come back to the fold. Think of your loneliness; even your sister is forsaking you. Your eyes are big with anguish, your face is pale and drawn. The disease you're suffering from is inhuman, foreign to my nature, foreign to yourself. Come back. I am forgetfulness, I am peace.

ORESTES: Foreign to myself—I know it. Outside nature, against nature, without excuse, beyond remedy, except what remedy I find within myself. But I shall not return under your law; I am doomed to have no other law but mine. Nor shall I come back to Nature, the Nature you found good; in it are a thousand beaten paths all leading up to you—but I must blaze my trail. For I, Zeus, am a man, and every man must find out his own way. Nature abhors man, and you too, god of gods, abhor mankind.

ZEUS: That is true; men like you I hold in abhorrence.

ORESTES: Take care; those words were a confession of your weakness. As for me, I do not hate you. What have I to do with you, or you with me? We shall glide past each other, like ships in a river, without touching. You are God and I am free; each of us is alone, and our anguish is akin. How can you know I did not try to feel remorse in the long night that has gone by? And to sleep? But no longer can I feel remorse, and I can sleep no more.

[*A short silence.*]

ZEUS: What do you propose to do?

ORESTES: The folk of Argos are my folk. I must open their eyes.

ZEUS: Poor people! Your gift to them will be a sad one; of loneliness and shame. You will tear from their eyes the veils I had laid on them, and they will see their lives as they are, foul and futile, a barren boon.

ORESTES: Why, since it is their lot, should I deny them the despair I have in me?

ZEUS: What will they make of it?

ORESTES: What they choose. They're free; and human life begins on the far side of despair.

[*A short silence.*]

ZEUS: Well, Orestes, all this was foreknown. In the fullness of time a man was to come, to announce my decline. And you're that man, it seems. But seeing you yesterday—you with your girlish face—who'd have believed it?

ORESTES: Could I myself have believed it? . . . The words I speak are too big for my mouth, they tear it; the load of destiny I bear is too heavy for my youth and has shattered it.

ZEUS: I have little love for you, yet I am sorry for you.

ORESTES: And I, too, am sorry for *you*.

ZEUS: Good-by, Orestes. [*He takes some steps forward.*] As for you, Electra, bear this in mind. My reign is not yet over—far from it!—and I shall not give up the struggle. So choose if you are with me or against me. Farewell.

ORESTES: Farewell. [ZEUS *goes out.* ELECTRA *slowly rises to her feet.*] Where are you going?

ELECTRA: Leave me alone. I'm done with you.

ORESTES: I have known you only for a day, and must I lose you now forever?

ELECTRA: Would to God that I had never known you!

ORESTES: Electra! My sister, dear Electra! My only love, the one joy of my life, do not leave me. Stay with me.

ELECTRA: Thief! I had so little, so very little to call mine; only a few weak dreams, a morsel of peace. And now you've taken my all; you've robbed a pauper of her mite! You were my brother, the head of our house, and it was your duty to protect me. But no, you needs must drag me into carnage; I am red as a flayed ox, these loathsome flies are swarming after me, and my heart is buzzing like an angry hive.

ORESTES: Yes, my beloved, it's true, I have taken all from you, and I have nothing to offer in return; nothing but my crime. But think how vast a gift that is! Believe me, it weighs on my heart like lead. We were too light, Electra; now our feet sink into the soil, like chariot-wheels in turf. So come with me; we will tread heavily on our way, bowed beneath our precious load. You shall give me your hand, and we will go—

ELECTRA: Where?

ORESTES: I don't know. Towards ourselves. Beyond the rivers and mountains are an Orestes and an Electra waiting for us, and we must make our patient way towards them.

ELECTRA: I won't hear any more from you. All you have to offer me is misery and squalor. [*She rushes out into the center of the stage. The* FURIES *slowly close in on her.*] Help! Zeus, king of gods and men, my king, take me in your arms, carry me from this place, and shelter me. I will obey your law, I will be your creature and your slave, I will embrace your knees. Save me from the flies, from my brother, from myself! Do not leave me lonely and I will give up my whole life to atonement. I repent, Zeus. I bitterly repent.

[*She runs off the stage. The* FURIES *make as if to follow her, but the* FIRST FURY *holds them back.*]

FIRST FURY: Let her be, sisters. She is not for us. But that man is ours, and ours, I think, for many a day. His little soul is stubborn. He will suffer for two.

[*Buzzing, the* FURIES *approach* ORESTES.]

ORESTES: I am alone, alone.

FIRST FURY: No, no, my sweet little murderer, I'm staying with you, and you'll see what merry games I'll think up to entertain you.

ORESTES: Alone until I die. And after that—?

FIRST FURY: Take heart, sisters, he is weakening. See how his eyes dilate. Soon his nerves will be throbbing like harp-strings, in exquisite arpeggios of terror.

SECOND FURY: And hunger will drive him from his sanctuary before long. Before nightfall we shall know how his blood tastes.

ORESTES: Poor Electra!

[*The* TUTOR *enters.*]

THE TUTOR: Master! Young master! Where are you? It's so dark one can't see a thing. I'm bringing you some food. The townspeople have surrounded the temple; there's no hope of escape by daylight. We shall have to try our chance when night comes. Meanwhile, eat this food to keep your strength up. [*The* FURIES *bar his way.*] Hey! Who are these?

More of those primitive myths! Ah, how I regret that pleasant land of Attica, where reason's always right.

ORESTES: Do not try to approach me, or they will tear you in pieces.

THE TUTOR: Gently now, my lovelies. See what I've brought you, some nice meat and fruit. Here you are! Let's hope it will calm you down.

ORESTES: So the people of Argos have gathered outside the temple, have they?

THE TUTOR: Indeed they have, and I can't say which are the fiercer, the thirstier for your blood: these charming young creatures here, or your worthy subjects.

ORESTES: Good. [*A short silence.*] Open that door.

THE TUTOR: Have you lost your wits? They're waiting behind it, and they're armed.

ORESTES: Do as I told you.

THE TUTOR: For once permit me, sir, to disobey your orders. I tell you, they will stone you. It's madness.

ORESTES: Old man, I am your master, and I order you to unbar that door.

[*The* TUTOR *opens one leaf of the double doors a few inches.*]

THE TUTOR: Oh dear! Oh dear!

ORESTES: Open both leaves.

[*The* TUTOR *half opens both leaves of the door and takes cover behind one of them. The* CROWD *surges forward, thrusting the doors wide open; then stops, bewildered, on the threshold. The stage is flooded with bright light. Shouts rise from the* CROWD:

"Away with him!" "Kill him!" "Stone him!"
"Tear him in pieces!"]

ORESTES [*who has not heard them*] : The sun!

THE CROWD: Murderer! Butcher! Blasphemer! We'll
tear you limb from limb. We'll pour molten lead into
your veins.

A WOMAN : I'll pluck out your eyes.

A MAN : I'll eat your gizzard!

ORESTES [*drawing himself up to his full height*] : So
here you are, my true and loyal subjects? I am Orestes, your King, son of Agamemnon, and this is my
coronation day. [*Exclamations of amazement, mut-
terings among the crowd.*] Ah, you are lowering
your tone? [*Complete silence.*] I know; you fear
me. Fifteen years ago to the day, another murderer
showed himself to you, his arms red to the elbows,
gloved in blood. But him you did not fear; you read
in his eyes that he was of your kind, he had not the
courage of his crimes. A crime that its doer disowns
becomes ownerless—no man's crime; that's how you
see it, isn't it? More like an accident than a crime?

So you welcomed the criminal as your King, and
that crime without an owner started prowling round
the city, whimpering like a dog that has lost its master. You see me, men of Argos, you understand that
my crime is wholly mine; I claim it as my own, for
all to know; it is my glory, my life's work, and you
can neither punish me nor pity me. That is why I fill
you with fear.

And yet, my people, I love you, and it was for

your sake that I killed. For your sake. I had come to claim my kingdom, and you would have none of me because I was not of your kind. Now I am of your kind, my subjects; there is a bond of blood between us, and I have earned my kingship over you.

As for your sins and your remorse, your night-fears, and the crime Ægistheus committed—all are mine, I take them all upon me. Fear your Dead no longer; they are *my* Dead. And, see, your faithful flies have left you and come to me. But have no fear, people of Argos. I shall not sit on my victim's throne or take the scepter in my blood-stained hands. A god offered it to me, and I said no. I wish to be a king without a kingdom, without subjects.

Farewell, my people. Try to reshape your lives. All here is new, all must begin anew. And for me, too, a new life is beginning. A strange life. . . .

Listen now to this tale. One summer there was a plague of rats in Scyros. It was like a foul disease; they soiled and nibbled everything, and the people of the city were at their wits' end. But one day a flute-player came to the city. He took his stand in the market-place. Like this. [ORESTES *rises to his feet.*] He began playing on his flute and all the rats came out and crowded round him. Then he started off, taking long strides—like this. [*He comes down from the pedestal.*] And he called to the people of Scyros: "Make way!" [*The* CROWD *makes way for him.*] And all the rats raised their heads and hesitated—as the flies are doing. Look! Look at the

◇◇

flies! Then all of sudden they followed in his train.
And the flute-player, with his rats, vanished forever.
Thus.

[*He strides out into the light. Shrieking, the* FURIES
fling themselves after him.]

CURTAIN

A NOTE ON THE TYPE IN WHICH
THIS BOOK IS SET

This book was set on the Linotype in Janson, a recutting made direct from the type cast from matrices made by Anton Janson some time between 1660 and 1687.

Of Janson's origin nothing is known. He may have been a relative of Justus Janson, a printer of Danish birth who practised in Leipzig from 1614 to 1635. Some time between 1657 and 1668 Anton Janson, a punch-cutter and type-founder, bought from the Leipzig printer Johann Erich Hahn the type-foundry which had formerly been a part of the printing house of M. Friedrich Lankisch. Janson's types were first shown in a specimen sheet issued at Leipzig about 1675.